Mastering
ETHICAL HACKING
Concepts, Techniques, and Applications

Nikhilesh Mishra,
Author

Website
https://www.nikhileshmishra.com

Copyright Information

Dedication

This book is lovingly dedicated to the cherished memory of my father, **Late Krishna Gopal Mishra**, and my mother**, Mrs. Vijay Kanti Mishra.** Their unwavering support, guidance, and love continue to inspire me.

Table of Contents

Author's Preface

Welcome to the captivating world of the knowledge we are about to explore! Within these pages, we invite you to embark on a journey that delves into the frontiers of information and understanding.

Charting the Path to Knowledge

Dive deep into the subjects we are about to explore as we unravel the intricate threads of innovation, creativity, and problem-solving. Whether you're a curious enthusiast, a seasoned professional, or an eager learner, this book serves as your gateway to gaining a deeper understanding.

Your Guiding Light

From the foundational principles of our chosen field to the advanced frontiers of its applications, we've meticulously crafted this book to be your trusted companion. Each chapter is an expedition, guided by expertise and filled with practical insights to empower you on your quest for knowledge.

What Awaits You

- **Illuminate the Origins:** Embark on a journey through the historical evolution of our chosen field, discovering key milestones that have paved the way for breakthroughs.

- **Demystify Complex Concepts:** Grasp the fundamental principles, navigate intricate concepts, and explore practical applications.

- **Mastery of the Craft:** Equip yourself with the skills and knowledge needed to excel in our chosen domain.

Your Journey Begins Here

As we embark on this enlightening journey together, remember that mastery is not just about knowledge but also the wisdom to apply it. Let each chapter be a stepping stone towards unlocking your potential, and let this book be your guide to becoming a true connoisseur of our chosen field.

So, turn the page, delve into the chapters, and immerse yourself in the world of knowledge. Let curiosity be your compass, and let the pursuit of understanding be your guide.

Begin your expedition now. Your quest for mastery awaits!

Sincerely,

Nikhilesh Mishra, Author

Chapter 1:

Introduction to Ethical Hacking

In the digital age, where information is a currency and technology permeates every aspect of our lives, the concept of security has never been more critical. In a world constantly under threat from cybercriminals, data breaches, and malicious hackers, there emerges a distinct breed of professionals who stand on the frontline of defense – ethical hackers.

"Introduction to Ethical Hacking" serves as our gateway into the fascinating realm of ethical hacking. This chapter is the first step on a journey that delves deep into the world of cybersecurity, exploring the minds and methods of those dedicated to safeguarding our digital landscapes.

In this chapter, we will define the scope and significance of ethical hacking, understanding its pivotal role in fortifying the digital realm. We'll navigate the intricate web of legal and ethical considerations that guide the actions of ethical hackers, shedding light on the delicate balance they must strike between protecting and probing.

Ethical hacking, often likened to the concept of a white-hatted vigilante, empowers individuals with the skills and knowledge to assess vulnerabilities, uncover threats, and strengthen digital fortresses. Join us as we embark on a journey that will equip you with the insights and ethical principles essential for mastering the art of ethical hacking.

Prepare to embark on a voyage into the world of ethical hacking, where curiosity is channeled into security, and the pursuit of knowledge becomes a shield against digital threats.

A. Definition and Scope of Ethical Hacking

In a rapidly evolving digital landscape, where the internet and technology underpin almost every facet of our lives, the need for robust cybersecurity measures has never been more critical. Amid the constant threat of cyberattacks, data breaches, and digital vulnerabilities, ethical hacking emerges as a powerful weapon in the arsenal of safeguarding our digital assets and personal information.

Defining Ethical Hacking

At its core, ethical hacking, often referred to as penetration testing or white-hat hacking, is a systematic and legally sanctioned process of probing computer systems, networks, applications, and digital infrastructure to identify vulnerabilities, weaknesses, and potential threats. The key distinction that sets ethical hacking apart from malicious hacking is the explicit permission and ethical framework within which it operates.

Ethical hackers, also known as "white hat" hackers, are individuals or cybersecurity professionals with specialized knowledge and skills in hacking techniques. However, their intentions are entirely benevolent: to uncover security flaws, gaps, and vulnerabilities before malicious hackers can exploit them. Ethical hackers are essentially the digital vigilantes of the cyber world, acting as protectors rather than perpetrators.

The Expansive Scope of Ethical Hacking

The scope of ethical hacking is as broad as the digital universe itself. It encompasses a wide array of activities and areas of interest, making it a multidisciplinary field with a profound impact on various aspects of cybersecurity and digital defense. Let's explore the diverse domains within the scope of ethical hacking:

1.   **Network Security:** Ethical hackers evaluate the security of networks, identifying weaknesses in firewalls, routers, and network infrastructure. They conduct penetration testing to ascertain if unauthorized access or data breaches are possible.

2.   **Web Application Security:** In this domain, ethical hackers assess the security of web applications, such as online banking systems, e-commerce websites, and social media platforms. They search for vulnerabilities like SQL injection,

cross-site scripting (XSS), and insecure authentication.

3.   **Wireless Network Security:** Ethical hackers examine the security of wireless networks, including Wi-Fi networks. They investigate encryption protocols, test for vulnerabilities, and assess the strength of access controls.

4.   **Mobile and IoT Security:** With the proliferation of mobile devices and the internet of things (IoT), ethical hackers explore the security of mobile apps and connected devices, identifying vulnerabilities that could be exploited.

5.   **Social Engineering Testing:** Ethical hackers simulate social engineering attacks to gauge an organization's susceptibility to tactics like phishing, pretexting, and baiting. They help educate employees on recognizing and defending against these attacks.

6.   **Operating System Security:** Ethical hackers analyze the security of operating systems, looking for misconfigurations, vulnerabilities, and potential weaknesses that could be exploited by attackers.

7.   **Cloud Security:** As more businesses adopt cloud computing, ethical hackers assess the security of cloud-based platforms and services to ensure that sensitive data remains protected.

8.   **IoT Device Security:** With the proliferation of

connected devices, ethical hackers investigate the security of IoT devices and their ecosystems, identifying vulnerabilities and weaknesses in the hardware and software.

9. **Physical Security Testing:** In some cases, ethical hackers may even engage in physical penetration testing, assessing the security of physical access controls, surveillance systems, and other aspects of physical security.

10. **Incident Response and Forensics:** Ethical hackers may assist organizations in responding to and recovering from cybersecurity incidents. They may also conduct digital forensics to investigate security breaches and gather evidence.

In essence, the scope of ethical hacking extends to any technology, system, or infrastructure where security is a concern. Its goal is to proactively identify and mitigate vulnerabilities, thereby fortifying digital defenses and safeguarding against the potential devastation of cyberattacks.

Ethical hacking is not just a profession; it's a mindset dedicated to the noble cause of protecting individuals, organizations, and society at large from the ever-present threats lurking in the digital shadows.

B. The Role of Ethical Hackers: Guardians of Digital Security

In an era where data breaches and cyber threats have become all too common, ethical hackers have emerged as the unsung heroes of the digital world. Their role is pivotal in defending against malicious actors and ensuring the integrity, confidentiality, and availability of digital assets. This chapter delves into the multifaceted role of ethical hackers, also known as white-hat hackers, and the invaluable contributions they make to the realm of cybersecurity.

Guardians of Digital Fortresses

Ethical hackers, armed with the same skill sets and knowledge as their malicious counterparts, utilize their expertise for the greater good. They are entrusted with the responsibility of probing digital systems, networks, and applications, not with the intention of causing harm, but rather to identify vulnerabilities before cybercriminals can exploit them. In essence, they act as guardians of digital fortresses, defending against potential threats.

Key Roles and Responsibilities

1.   **Vulnerability Assessment:** Ethical hackers conduct systematic assessments of systems, networks, and software to uncover weaknesses and vulnerabilities. This process involves extensive testing and analysis to ensure that no potential entry points are left unexamined.

2.   **Penetration Testing:** Penetration testing, often referred to as pen testing, involves simulating cyberattacks to assess the resilience of a system's defenses. Ethical hackers attempt to breach security measures in controlled environments to identify weaknesses that require fortification.

3.   **Security Auditing:** Ethical hackers perform comprehensive security audits, examining an organization's digital infrastructure to ensure compliance with security standards, best practices, and regulatory requirements. These audits help organizations identify gaps in their security posture.

4.   **Incident Response:** Ethical hackers play a vital role in incident response teams. When a security incident occurs, they utilize their expertise to investigate the breach, contain the damage, and gather evidence for further action.

5.   **Security Advisory:** Ethical hackers provide expert guidance and recommendations to organizations on how to strengthen their cybersecurity posture. They offer actionable insights to mitigate risks and improve security measures.

6.   **Education and Awareness:** Ethical hackers are often involved in training and educating staff and organizations about cybersecurity best practices. They teach employees how to recognize and respond to potential threats, such as phishing attacks and social engineering.

7.   **Research and Development:** Many ethical hackers are engaged in ongoing research and development efforts to stay ahead of emerging threats and vulnerabilities. They contribute to the development of new security tools and techniques.

Ethical Considerations

Ethical hackers operate within a strict code of ethics, guided by principles that prioritize legality, integrity, and responsible disclosure. They obtain explicit permission from system owners before conducting any tests, ensuring that their actions are lawful and consensual.

Moreover, ethical hackers adhere to a responsibility of full disclosure. When they uncover vulnerabilities, they report their findings to the responsible parties, allowing them to take remedial action. This responsible disclosure prevents potential harm and fosters a collaborative approach to cybersecurity.

The Evolving Role

As the cybersecurity landscape continues to evolve, the role of ethical hackers expands in tandem. They face new challenges in securing emerging technologies, such as IoT devices, cloud computing, and artificial intelligence. Additionally, ethical hackers must adapt to the ever-changing tactics of cybercriminals, staying vigilant to protect against advanced threats.

In conclusion, ethical hackers are the unsung heroes of the digital age, defending against threats that imperil the security of individuals, organizations, and society as a whole. Their role is not just a profession; it is a mission to safeguard the digital realm and ensure that technology remains a force for good in our interconnected world.

C. Benefits and Challenges of Ethical Hacking: Navigating the Cybersecurity Landscape

Ethical hacking, as a proactive approach to cybersecurity, offers a wealth of benefits while presenting practitioners with a unique set of challenges. Understanding both the advantages and obstacles inherent to this field is essential for individuals and organizations seeking to harness the power of ethical hacking effectively.

Benefits of Ethical Hacking

1. **Identification of Vulnerabilities:** Ethical hackers play a critical role in identifying vulnerabilities and weaknesses in systems, networks, and applications. By uncovering these issues before malicious hackers do, organizations can address them promptly, thereby reducing the risk of cyberattacks and data breaches.

2. **Enhanced Security Posture:** Through continuous

testing and evaluation, ethical hacking helps organizations enhance their security posture. This proactive approach enables them to stay one step ahead of cyber threats and adapt to evolving attack techniques.

3. **Cost Savings:** Identifying and addressing security vulnerabilities early in the development or operational phases is more cost-effective than dealing with the consequences of a successful cyberattack. Ethical hacking can lead to significant cost savings by preventing potential breaches.

4. **Compliance and Regulation:** Many industries and regulatory bodies require organizations to undergo regular security assessments and audits. Ethical hacking assists organizations in meeting compliance requirements and adhering to data protection laws.

5. **Protection of Reputation:** A successful cyberattack can have devastating consequences for an organization's reputation. Ethical hacking helps prevent security incidents, safeguarding the trust and confidence of customers, partners, and stakeholders.

6. **Educational Value:** Ethical hacking promotes cybersecurity education and awareness. It empowers IT professionals and organizations with knowledge about the latest threats and best practices, fostering a culture of security.

7.   **Incident Response Preparation:** Ethical hackers assist organizations in preparing for potential incidents. By simulating cyberattacks, they help organizations develop effective incident response plans, minimizing the impact of security breaches.

Challenges of Ethical Hacking

1.   **Legal and Ethical Dilemmas:** Ethical hackers must navigate a complex legal and ethical landscape. They must obtain explicit permission to test systems, and their actions must comply with local and international laws. The boundaries between ethical hacking and malicious hacking can be blurry, requiring careful ethical considerations.

2.   **Skill and Knowledge Requirements:** Ethical hacking demands a high level of technical expertise and continuous learning. Staying up-to-date with the latest hacking techniques, tools, and security trends is a constant challenge.

3.   **Resource Intensiveness:** Ethical hacking can be resource-intensive, both in terms of time and financial investment. Organizations need to allocate resources for training, tools, and ongoing testing.

4.   **False Positives and Negatives:** Ethical hackers may encounter false positives (indications of vulnerabilities that do not exist) and false negatives (missed vulnerabilities). Distinguishing

between genuine threats and false alarms requires expertise.

5.   **Impact on Systems:** In some cases, penetration testing or vulnerability scanning may unintentionally disrupt systems or services. Ethical hackers must carefully plan their activities to minimize any negative impact.

6.   **Evolving Threat Landscape:** The cybersecurity landscape is constantly evolving, with new threats emerging regularly. Ethical hackers must adapt to stay ahead of cybercriminals and continuously refine their skills.

7.   **Limited Visibility:** Ethical hackers can only assess what is within their scope of engagement. This limitation means that some vulnerabilities outside the scope may remain undiscovered.

In summary, ethical hacking offers organizations a proactive and effective means of strengthening their cybersecurity defenses, protecting sensitive data, and complying with regulatory requirements. However, it comes with its share of challenges, including legal and ethical considerations, resource requirements, and the ever-changing nature of cybersecurity threats. To harness the benefits of ethical hacking while mitigating these challenges, organizations should approach it with a well-defined strategy and a commitment to ongoing education and improvement.

Chapter 2:

Understanding Cybersecurity

In our interconnected and digital age, where information flows seamlessly across networks, and transactions occur at the speed of thought, the concept of cybersecurity has risen to paramount importance. As our reliance on technology deepens, so too does the need for robust defenses against the ever-present and evolving threats that lurk in the digital shadows.

"Understanding Cybersecurity" serves as a beacon of illumination in the complex and dynamic landscape of digital security. This chapter is the gateway to a journey that delves deep into the heart of cybersecurity, exploring the fundamental principles, threats, and strategies that underpin our ability to protect digital assets.

In this chapter, we will embark on a voyage of discovery, unveiling the essential concepts that form the bedrock of cybersecurity. We will explore the multifaceted nature of cyber threats, from the subtle nuances of social engineering to the intricate mechanisms of sophisticated malware. Along the way, we will delve into the foundational principles of the CIA Triad (Confidentiality, Integrity, Availability) and the critical role it plays in shaping security policies and standards.

Cybersecurity, in its essence, is not just a technological endeavor; it is a holistic approach to safeguarding our digital way of life. It demands an understanding of human behavior, a mastery of cutting-edge technologies, and an unwavering commitment to protecting the digital infrastructure that underpins modern society.

As we embark on this exploration of cybersecurity, prepare to gain the knowledge and insights necessary to navigate the intricate web of threats and countermeasures that define our interconnected world. Join us as we journey deeper into the realm of cybersecurity, where vigilance and understanding are the keys to a safer digital future.

A. Fundamentals of Cybersecurity: Building Blocks of Digital Defense

In the age of digitization, where information is the lifeblood of businesses and individuals alike, cybersecurity stands as the guardian of our digital world. To grasp the complexities and nuances of cybersecurity, one must first establish a firm foundation in its fundamentals. This chapter serves as the cornerstone, where we unravel the key principles, concepts, and strategies that underpin the art and science of safeguarding our digital assets.

The CIA Triad: Pillars of Cybersecurity

At the heart of cybersecurity lies the CIA Triad, a foundational concept that encapsulates the core objectives of information security:

1.   **Confidentiality:** This pillar emphasizes the protection of sensitive data from unauthorized access or disclosure. In essence, it ensures that information is only accessible to those with the appropriate permissions. Encryption, access controls, and data classification are among the tools and techniques employed to uphold confidentiality.

2.   **Integrity:** Integrity revolves around maintaining the accuracy and reliability of data. It ensures that information is protected from unauthorized alterations, ensuring its trustworthiness. Techniques such as data hashing and digital signatures help verify data integrity.

3.   **Availability:** Availability ensures that information and resources are accessible and usable when needed. Cybersecurity measures, such as redundancy, fault tolerance, and disaster recovery planning, aim to minimize downtime and guarantee resource availability.

Security Models and Policies

To translate the principles of the CIA Triad into actionable strategies, organizations rely on security models and policies:

1.   **Access Control Models:** These models define how users and systems can access resources. Common models include discretionary access control (DAC), mandatory access control (MAC), and role-based access control (RBAC).

2.   **Security Policies:** Security policies are the cornerstone of a cybersecurity strategy. They lay out guidelines, rules, and procedures that dictate how an organization should protect its assets. Policies cover a wide range of areas, including data handling, network security, and incident response.

Threats and Attack Vectors

Understanding the fundamentals of cybersecurity also entails recognizing the spectrum of threats and attack vectors:

1.   **Malware:** Malicious software, including viruses, worms, Trojans, and ransomware, poses a constant threat. These programs are designed to compromise the confidentiality, integrity, or availability of data and systems.

2.   **Phishing:** Social engineering attacks, such as phishing, rely on manipulating human psychology to trick individuals into divulging sensitive information or downloading malicious software.

3.   **Denial of Service (DoS) Attacks:** These attacks aim

to disrupt the availability of services or resources, rendering them inaccessible to legitimate users.

4. **Insider Threats:** Sometimes, threats come from within an organization. Insiders with malicious intent can compromise security, highlighting the importance of access controls and monitoring.

5. **Advanced Persistent Threats (APTs):** APTs are sophisticated and long-term cyberattacks that often target high-value assets. They require vigilant monitoring and response.

Risk Management

Fundamental to cybersecurity is risk management. Organizations must assess, mitigate, and manage risks to protect their digital assets effectively. This includes identifying vulnerabilities, assessing their potential impact, and implementing controls to reduce risks.

Continuous Learning and Adaptation

Cybersecurity is not static; it's an ever-evolving field. Threats, technologies, and attack vectors change rapidly. As such, a fundamental aspect of cybersecurity is the commitment to continuous learning and adaptation. Cybersecurity professionals must stay updated with the latest threats and security measures to remain effective in their roles.

In conclusion, the fundamentals of cybersecurity are the building blocks upon which effective digital defense is constructed. The CIA Triad, security models, policies, threat awareness, and risk management form the bedrock of a robust cybersecurity strategy. Armed with this understanding, organizations and individuals can embark on the journey toward securing their digital environments in an increasingly interconnected world.

B. Threats and Attack Vectors: Unveiling the Digital Perils

In the ever-evolving realm of cybersecurity, the landscape is fraught with threats and attack vectors that pose a constant and formidable challenge. To build a robust defense, one must comprehend the diverse array of adversaries and techniques lurking in the digital shadows. This chapter serves as an expedition into the heart of cybersecurity threats, unearthing the multifaceted dangers and vulnerabilities that organizations and individuals face.

Malware: Silent Intruders

At the forefront of cybersecurity threats stands malware, a portmanteau of "malicious software." Malware encompasses a vast spectrum of insidious programs, each with a specific modus operandi:

1.   **Viruses:** These programs attach themselves to legitimate files and replicate when the infected file is executed. Viruses can corrupt, steal, or delete data.

2.   **Worms:** Unlike viruses, worms are self-replicating and spread independently. They exploit vulnerabilities in software or network protocols to propagate rapidly.

3.   **Trojans:** Named after the Trojan Horse of Greek mythology, Trojans disguise themselves as legitimate software but harbor malicious payloads. They often create backdoors for remote access or steal sensitive information.

4.   **Ransomware:** This infamous breed of malware encrypts files and demands a ransom for decryption keys. It has wreaked havoc on organizations worldwide.

5.   **Spyware:** Spyware clandestinely monitors a user's activities and gathers sensitive information, such as login credentials and browsing history.

6.   **Adware:** While less malicious, adware inundates users with unwanted advertisements and may lead to privacy breaches.

Phishing: The Art of Deception

Phishing, a form of social engineering, relies on deception to manipulate individuals into divulging sensitive information or taking harmful actions:

1.   **Email Phishing:** Attackers send fraudulent emails that appear legitimate, often with malicious links or attachments. They impersonate trusted entities, urging recipients to click or provide personal information.

2.   **Spear Phishing:** A targeted form of phishing, spear phishing tailors attacks to specific individuals or organizations. Attackers craft convincing messages based on extensive research.

3.   **Smishing and Vishing:** Phishing extends beyond email to text messages (smishing) and voice calls (vishing), where attackers impersonate legitimate entities or use scare tactics to deceive victims.

Denial of Service (DoS) and Distributed Denial of Service (DDoS) Attacks: Availability Under Siege

DoS and DDoS attacks aim to disrupt the availability of services, networks, or websites:

1.   **DoS Attacks:** A single source overwhelms a target with excessive traffic, rendering it unavailable to legitimate users.

2.   **DDoS Attacks:** Multiple sources, often a botnet, flood a target with traffic, making it extremely challenging to mitigate.

Insider Threats: The Enemy Within

While external threats are well-documented, insider threats

come from individuals within an organization:

1. **Malicious Insiders:** Employees or associates with access to sensitive data or systems may abuse their privileges for personal gain or to harm the organization.

2. **Negligent Insiders:** Employees who inadvertently compromise security through actions such as careless data handling or falling victim to phishing attacks.

Advanced Persistent Threats (APTs): Silent, Persistent Intruders

APTs are highly sophisticated, long-term cyberattacks typically targeting high-value assets. They may involve:

1. **Stealthy Intrusion:** APTs focus on remaining undetected for extended periods, often using zero-day vulnerabilities.

2. **Data Exfiltration:** Attackers gradually exfiltrate sensitive data over time, causing prolonged harm.

Zero-Day Exploits: The Unknown Vulnerabilities

Zero-day exploits target undisclosed vulnerabilities in software or hardware. These vulnerabilities are not known to the vendor or the public, making them highly dangerous.

Physical Attacks: Tangible Threats

Physical security threats involve tangible actions, such as:

1.   **Unauthorized Access:** Attackers physically breach secure areas or gain access to hardware, potentially compromising data or systems.

2.   **Device Theft:** Theft of laptops, mobile devices, or other hardware can result in data breaches or unauthorized access.

In conclusion, comprehending the diverse threats and attack vectors in cybersecurity is paramount to developing effective defenses. Organizations and individuals must remain vigilant, continually updating their knowledge and cybersecurity measures to thwart these pernicious adversaries. Cybersecurity is a dynamic battlefield, and knowledge is the most potent weapon in the fight to secure the digital realm.

C. Security Models (CIA Triad): Safeguarding the Essence of Information Security

In the realm of information security, the foremost concern is the protection of data and digital assets against an array of threats. Security models provide a structured framework for achieving this goal. At the heart of these models is the CIA Triad—a fundamental concept that encapsulates the core principles of information security: Confidentiality, Integrity, and Availability.

The CIA Triad: Cornerstone of Information Security

The CIA Triad is a triumvirate of principles that serves as the bedrock of information security:

1.   **Confidentiality:** This pillar emphasizes the protection of sensitive data from unauthorized access or disclosure. It ensures that information is only accessible to those with the appropriate permissions. Confidentiality aims to maintain the privacy and secrecy of data.

•   **Access Controls:** Access controls, including authentication and authorization mechanisms, play a pivotal role in preserving confidentiality. They ensure that only authorized users can access sensitive data.

•   **Encryption:** Data encryption transforms information into an unreadable format without the correct decryption key, rendering it useless to unauthorized parties.

2.   **Integrity:** Integrity revolves around maintaining the accuracy and reliability of data. It ensures that information is protected from unauthorized alterations, preserving its trustworthiness.

•   **Data Hashing:** Hash functions generate unique fixed-length strings (hashes) for data. Any change in the data, no matter how small, results in a significantly different hash, making it easy to detect tampering.

- **Digital Signatures:** Digital signatures use cryptographic techniques to verify the authenticity and integrity of data. They confirm that the data has not been altered since it was signed.

3. **Availability:** Availability ensures that information and resources are accessible and usable when needed. Cybersecurity measures aim to minimize downtime and guarantee the availability of resources, even in the face of threats.

- **Redundancy:** Redundant systems and failover mechanisms ensure that services remain available in the event of hardware or software failures.

- **Disaster Recovery:** Disaster recovery plans and backups safeguard data against loss and facilitate rapid recovery in case of disasters.

Security Models: Applying the Triad

Security models provide a structured approach to implementing the CIA Triad principles:

1. **Access Control Models:** Access control models define how users and systems can access resources. These models play a crucial role in enforcing the confidentiality and availability aspects of the CIA Triad.

- **Discretionary Access Control (DAC):** DAC grants users control over the access to their objects, allowing them to set permissions. It is common in home and small business environments.

- **Mandatory Access Control (MAC):** MAC enforces access controls based on labels and security clearances. It is prevalent in government and military environments.

- **Role-Based Access Control (RBAC):** RBAC assigns roles to users and grants permissions based on those roles. It simplifies access management and is used in various industries.

2. **Security Policies:** Security policies are the guiding principles and rules that an organization follows to safeguard information. They translate the CIA Triad into actionable strategies and encompass various areas, including data handling, network security, and incident response.

- **Data Handling Policies:** These policies outline how data should be classified, stored, transmitted, and disposed of securely.

- **Network Security Policies:** Network security policies define rules for network access, firewall configurations, and intrusion detection/prevention.

- **Incident Response Policies:** These policies outline

procedures for detecting, reporting, and mitigating security incidents.

The Evolving Landscape

The CIA Triad and associated security models are not static concepts; they adapt to the evolving cybersecurity landscape. Emerging technologies, such as cloud computing and the Internet of Things (IoT), introduce new challenges and considerations for information security. Additionally, as threats continue to evolve, security models and practices must evolve to address them effectively.

In conclusion, security models, guided by the CIA Triad, form the cornerstone of information security. They provide a structured framework for organizations and individuals to protect data and digital assets against a wide range of threats. Adherence to these principles is essential in maintaining the confidentiality, integrity, and availability of information in an increasingly interconnected and data-driven world.

D. Security Policies and Standards: The Blueprint for Cyber Resilience

In the dynamic landscape of information security, security policies and standards serve as the North Star guiding organizations through the intricacies of safeguarding data and digital assets. These documents establish a framework of rules, guidelines, and best practices that are essential for protecting sensitive information, maintaining compliance, and ensuring the resilience of digital ecosystems.

Security Policies: Defining the Rules of Engagement

Security policies are the foundational documents that outline an organization's approach to information security. They establish a set of rules, procedures, and expectations that govern how employees, contractors, and third parties interact with information systems and data. Security policies are vital for several reasons:

1.   **Risk Management:** Security policies provide a structured approach to identifying, assessing, and mitigating risks associated with information security. By defining acceptable behaviors and security controls, they help protect sensitive data from threats and vulnerabilities.

2.   **Compliance:** Many industries and regulatory bodies require organizations to adhere to specific security standards and practices. Security policies ensure compliance with these legal and regulatory requirements, reducing the risk of fines and legal consequences.

3.   **Consistency:** Security policies promote consistency in security practices across an organization. They set clear expectations for all stakeholders, ensuring that security measures

are applied uniformly.

4.   **Incident Response:** In the event of a security incident, well-defined policies guide the organization's response. They dictate how to detect, report, and remediate security breaches, minimizing damage and recovery time.

Types of Security Policies

Security policies encompass a wide range of areas within an organization's information security framework. Some of the most common types include:

1.   **Data Handling Policy:** This policy defines how sensitive data is classified, stored, transmitted, and disposed of. It specifies who has access to various types of data and under what conditions.

2.   **Access Control Policy:** Access control policies outline the rules governing user access to information systems and resources. They detail authentication mechanisms, authorization levels, and user roles.

3.   **Network Security Policy:** Network security policies dictate the rules for securing an organization's network infrastructure. This includes firewall configurations, intrusion detection/prevention systems, and encryption standards.

4.   **Incident Response Policy:** This policy outlines the

procedures for detecting, reporting, and responding to security incidents. It defines roles and responsibilities during incident handling.

5.   **Acceptable Use Policy:** Acceptable use policies specify how employees and other stakeholders are allowed to use company resources, including computers, networks, and internet access. They often address personal device usage and internet browsing.

Security Standards: Detailed Implementation Guidance

While security policies provide the overarching framework, security standards offer more granular, detailed guidelines for implementing specific security controls. These standards align with the policies and provide step-by-step instructions for implementing security measures effectively. Security standards are beneficial for the following reasons:

1.   **Technical Guidance:** Security standards offer specific, technical instructions for configuring and maintaining security controls. They help ensure that security measures are implemented correctly.

2.   **Interoperability:** Standards ensure that security controls are compatible with each other and with industry best practices. This promotes a cohesive and comprehensive security posture.

3.   **Compliance:** Security standards often align with industry regulations and frameworks. Following recognized standards can facilitate compliance efforts and simplify auditing processes.

Examples of Security Standards

Various organizations and standards bodies publish security standards to guide organizations in securing their information systems. Some well-known security standards include:

1.   **ISO/IEC 27001:** The ISO/IEC 27001 standard provides a framework for establishing, implementing, maintaining, and continually improving an information security management system (ISMS). It covers a broad range of security controls and best practices.

2.   **NIST Cybersecurity Framework:** Developed by the National Institute of Standards and Technology (NIST), this framework offers guidelines for managing and reducing cybersecurity risk. It consists of five core functions: Identify, Protect, Detect, Respond, and Recover.

3.   **PCI DSS:** The Payment Card Industry Data Security Standard (PCI DSS) outlines security requirements for organizations that handle credit card data. It includes specific controls for securing payment card data and systems.

Implementation and Enforcement

To derive maximum benefit from security policies and standards, organizations must follow a systematic approach:

1.   **Development:** Begin by developing comprehensive security policies tailored to the organization's specific needs, risks, and compliance requirements.

2.   **Communication:** Ensure that all stakeholders, including employees, contractors, and third parties, are aware of and understand the policies and standards.

3.   **Training:** Provide training and awareness programs to educate employees about security policies and standards, including their roles and responsibilities.

4.   **Enforcement:** Implement mechanisms to enforce security policies, including access controls, monitoring, and compliance audits.

5.   **Review and Updates:** Regularly review and update security policies and standards to adapt to evolving threats, technologies, and regulatory changes.

In conclusion, security policies and standards form the backbone of a robust information security program. They provide organizations with a structured approach to protecting sensitive data, mitigating risks, and ensuring compliance with legal and regulatory requirements. By aligning policies and standards with industry best practices, organizations can build a resilient security posture in an increasingly complex and interconnected digital landscape.

Chapter 3:

Ethical Hacking Methodology

In the realm of cybersecurity, where the stakes are high and the adversaries relentless, success hinges on a well-defined and systematic approach. The chapter on "Ethical Hacking Methodology" unveils the blueprint that ethical hackers follow as they embark on the challenging journey of probing, testing, and safeguarding digital fortresses.

Ethical hacking, at its core, is a carefully choreographed dance between offense and defense—a calculated exploration of vulnerabilities and exploits, all executed with the utmost responsibility and legality. This chapter illuminates the intricate steps of this dance, providing aspiring ethical hackers with the tools, techniques, and mindset necessary to uncover weaknesses before malicious adversaries can exploit them.

In the pages that follow, we will traverse the phases of ethical hacking methodology, from the initial reconnaissance and information gathering to the critical steps of vulnerability assessment, exploitation, and post-exploitation. Each stage is a critical piece of the puzzle, allowing ethical hackers to meticulously assess, fortify, and report on the security posture of systems, networks, and applications.

In a world where cyber threats continue to evolve in sophistication and scale, ethical hacking methodology stands as a beacon of defense—a powerful approach that enables us to remain one step ahead of the digital adversaries. As we journey through this chapter, be prepared to unravel the secrets of ethical hacking, mastering the art of probing the digital realm while adhering to the highest ethical standards.

A. Reconnaissance and Information Gathering: The Art of Digital Espionage

In the intricate realm of ethical hacking, the initial phase of reconnaissance and information gathering sets the stage for the entire operation. Often likened to the reconnaissance carried out by spies in the physical world, this phase is the digital equivalent—a meticulous process of gathering intelligence about a target, understanding its vulnerabilities, and charting a course of action. Ethical hackers, armed with curiosity and an analytical mindset, embark on this journey to uncover the hidden secrets of systems, networks, and applications.

The Pillars of Reconnaissance

Reconnaissance consists of two primary categories: passive and active reconnaissance.

1.	**Passive Reconnaissance:** In this initial phase, ethical hackers collect information without directly interacting with the target. The goal is to assemble a comprehensive profile of the target's digital footprint. Techniques include:

- 	**Open-Source Intelligence (OSINT):** OSINT involves scouring publicly available information from sources like websites, social media, and public records. Ethical hackers analyze data such as domain registration records, DNS information, and historical website content.

- 	**Google Dorking:** Google Dorking is a technique that leverages advanced search operators to identify sensitive information and vulnerabilities exposed on the internet.

- 	**Social Engineering:** Ethical hackers may use social engineering techniques to gather information from employees or individuals associated with the target. This can include phishing emails or pretexting phone calls.

2.	**Active Reconnaissance:** Once a foundation of information is established, active reconnaissance involves more direct interactions with the target. The objective is to validate and expand on the information gathered passively. Techniques include:

- 	**Port Scanning:** Port scanning involves sending packets to target systems to determine which network ports are open and what services are running. Tools like Nmap are commonly used for this purpose.

• **Network Mapping:** Ethical hackers create a map of the target's network, identifying key assets, servers, and their interconnections. This provides insight into the target's infrastructure.

• **Vulnerability Scanning:** Vulnerability scanners like Nessus or OpenVAS are employed to identify potential vulnerabilities in the target's systems and applications.

The Art of Enumeration

Enumeration is a critical aspect of the reconnaissance phase. It involves extracting specific information about the target, such as user accounts, system details, and network shares. The process often begins with information obtained through passive and active reconnaissance and progresses to more detailed probing.

1. **Service Enumeration:** Ethical hackers identify the services running on target systems and gather information about their versions and configurations. This helps in pinpointing potential vulnerabilities.

2. **OS Fingerprinting:** OS fingerprinting is the process of determining the operating system of target systems. This information is valuable for crafting attacks tailored to the specific

OS.

3.   **Exploiting Vulnerabilities:** In some cases, ethical hackers may discover vulnerabilities during the reconnaissance and enumeration phases. While exploitation typically occurs later in the ethical hacking methodology, these findings inform the overall strategy.

The Value of Reconnaissance

The reconnaissance and information gathering phase may appear subtle, but its significance cannot be overstated:

1.   **Risk Assessment:** By understanding the target's digital footprint and potential vulnerabilities, ethical hackers can assess the level of risk associated with the target and prioritize their efforts accordingly.

2.   **Tailored Attacks:** The information gathered informs the selection and customization of attack vectors. Ethical hackers can craft attacks that are more likely to succeed based on their knowledge of the target's systems and infrastructure.

3.   **Minimizing Footprints:** Ethical hackers aim to conduct reconnaissance quietly and without alerting the target. This clandestine approach minimizes the risk of detection and disruption.

4.   **Legal and Ethical Compliance:** Ethical hackers must

ensure that their reconnaissance activities remain within legal and ethical boundaries. Unauthorized access to systems or networks is strictly prohibited.

In conclusion, the reconnaissance and information gathering phase is the foundational step in ethical hacking methodology. It is a strategic blend of passive and active techniques aimed at uncovering the digital secrets of a target. Ethical hackers rely on this phase to gather intelligence, assess risks, and tailor their approach to uncover vulnerabilities, all while adhering to strict legal and ethical standards.

B. Scanning and Enumeration: Probing the Digital Landscape

As the ethical hacking journey progresses, the phases of scanning and enumeration emerge as critical milestones in the quest to uncover vulnerabilities and assess the security posture of a target system or network. These phases build upon the foundation laid during reconnaissance, diving deeper into the digital landscape to identify open ports, services, and potential weaknesses.

Scanning: Uncovering the Network Blueprint

Scanning involves probing the target system or network to identify open ports, services, and active hosts. Ethical hackers use specialized tools and techniques to systematically scan the target, often classified as follows:

1.   **Port Scanning:** This is the process of identifying open network ports on a target system. Open ports indicate services that are actively listening for connections. Ethical hackers use tools like Nmap to perform port scans, revealing potential entry points into the target.

•   **TCP Connect Scanning:** This method establishes a full connection to each port to determine its status (open, closed, or filtered).

•   **UDP Scanning:** UDP scans probe open UDP ports, which are commonly used for services that do not require a connection-oriented protocol.

•   **Stealth Scanning:** Techniques like SYN scanning (also known as half-open scanning) minimize the footprint of the scan and can evade some intrusion detection systems (IDS).

2.   **Service Identification:** Once open ports are discovered, ethical hackers aim to identify the services running on those ports. Tools like banner grabbing and service fingerprinting help determine the type and version of services, potentially revealing known vulnerabilities.

3.   **Operating System Detection:** Ethical hackers use OS

fingerprinting techniques to determine the target's operating system. Knowing the OS is valuable for crafting targeted exploits.

Enumeration: Extracting Valuable Data

Enumeration is the process of actively extracting information about the target system or network. It involves querying identified services for additional details, such as user accounts, shares, and system configurations. Key aspects of enumeration include:

1. **User Enumeration:** Ethical hackers probe for information about user accounts, such as usernames, group memberships, and account policies. User enumeration can be crucial for subsequent phases, such as password cracking and privilege escalation.

2. **Network Share Enumeration:** Identifying shared resources on the network, such as file shares and printers, can reveal potential points of entry or sensitive information exposure.

3. **SNMP Enumeration:** Simple Network Management Protocol (SNMP) enumeration involves querying network devices for information about their configurations and status. SNMP can provide insights into network architecture.

4. **DNS Enumeration:** Enumeration of Domain Name System (DNS) information can yield details about the target's domain structure, subdomains, and mail servers.

The Value of Scanning and Enumeration

The scanning and enumeration phases are not merely technical exercises; they serve vital purposes within the ethical hacking methodology:

1.   **Risk Assessment:** These phases provide ethical hackers with a deeper understanding of the target's infrastructure, allowing for a more precise risk assessment. Vulnerabilities and weaknesses become more apparent.

2.   **Exploitation Planning:** Armed with information about open ports, services, and potential vulnerabilities, ethical hackers can develop targeted exploit strategies.

3.   **Network Mapping:** Scanning and enumeration contribute to network mapping, helping ethical hackers understand the layout and interconnectedness of the target network.

4.   **Privilege Escalation:** User enumeration is particularly valuable for identifying potential points of privilege escalation. Ethical hackers can identify users with elevated privileges and potential misconfigurations.

Legal and Ethical Considerations

Ethical hackers must conduct scanning and enumeration activities within strict legal and ethical boundaries. Unauthorized access or disruption of systems and networks is prohibited and could have legal consequences.

In conclusion, the scanning and enumeration phases are essential components of ethical hacking methodology, allowing ethical hackers to explore the digital landscape of target systems and networks. These phases provide valuable insights into vulnerabilities, service configurations, and potential points of entry, all of which are instrumental in crafting targeted exploit strategies and enhancing the overall security posture of the target. Ethical hackers approach these activities with precision, diligence, and a strict adherence to legal and ethical standards.

C. Vulnerability Assessment: Unveiling Weaknesses in the Digital Armor

In the realm of ethical hacking, the phase of vulnerability assessment takes center stage as ethical hackers meticulously examine the target system or network for weaknesses and security vulnerabilities. This critical phase not only uncovers potential points of exploitation but also serves as a proactive measure to fortify an organization's digital defenses.

The Essence of Vulnerability Assessment

Vulnerability assessment is the process of identifying, quantifying, and prioritizing vulnerabilities within a target system or network. It is a systematic and methodical examination, often employing a combination of automated scanning tools and manual analysis. The objectives of this phase include:

1.   **Identification:** Ethical hackers seek to identify vulnerabilities, which can range from software flaws and misconfigurations to weak passwords and open ports.

2.   **Quantification:** Each identified vulnerability is assessed to determine its potential impact and risk. This quantification helps prioritize which vulnerabilities should be addressed first.

3.   **Prioritization:** Vulnerabilities are ranked based on their severity, potential impact, and likelihood of exploitation. High-priority vulnerabilities demand immediate attention.

4.   **Documentation:** Ethical hackers maintain detailed records of identified vulnerabilities, including their descriptions, risk ratings, and recommendations for mitigation.

Techniques and Tools

Vulnerability assessment employs a variety of techniques and tools to achieve its objectives:

1.   **Automated Scanning Tools:** Vulnerability scanners, such as Nessus, OpenVAS, and Qualys, automate the process of identifying vulnerabilities by scanning target systems and

networks for known weaknesses.

2. **Manual Analysis:** Ethical hackers often complement automated scans with manual analysis to identify vulnerabilities that may not be detected by scanning tools. This includes code review, configuration analysis, and other hands-on approaches.

3. **Threat Modeling:** Threat modeling is a proactive approach to identifying potential vulnerabilities by examining the system's design and architecture. It helps anticipate and prevent security issues.

Common Vulnerabilities Targeted

During a vulnerability assessment, ethical hackers scrutinize a wide range of common vulnerabilities, including but not limited to:

1. **Software Vulnerabilities:** These include known vulnerabilities in operating systems, applications, and libraries. Patches and updates are essential for addressing these issues.

2. **Misconfigurations:** Improperly configured systems, services, or firewalls can create security weaknesses. Ethical hackers look for misconfigured settings that may expose sensitive information or services.

3. **Weak Authentication:** Vulnerabilities related to weak or default passwords, insufficient password policies, or unsecured

authentication mechanisms are high-priority targets.

4.   **Unpatched Systems:** Failure to apply security patches and updates can leave systems vulnerable to known exploits. Ethical hackers verify that systems are up to date.

5.   **Open Ports and Services:** Any open ports or services that are not necessary for the operation of the system are potential entry points for attackers.

Risk Assessment and Reporting

Once vulnerabilities are identified, ethical hackers assess their potential impact on the organization's security. This assessment includes considering the likelihood of exploitation, the level of access an attacker could gain, and the potential consequences of a successful attack.

Ethical hackers then compile their findings into detailed vulnerability assessment reports. These reports typically include:

1.   **Vulnerability Descriptions:** Clear and concise descriptions of each identified vulnerability.

2.   **Risk Ratings:** Vulnerabilities are assigned risk ratings based on their severity, potential impact, and likelihood of exploitation.

3.   **Recommendations:** Specific recommendations for

mitigating each vulnerability. This may include applying patches, reconfiguring systems, or implementing additional security measures.

4.   **Prioritization:** A prioritized list of vulnerabilities, indicating which should be addressed first based on their risk ratings.

The Value of Vulnerability Assessment

Vulnerability assessment serves as a critical checkpoint in the ethical hacking methodology:

1.   **Risk Mitigation:** By identifying vulnerabilities and providing recommendations for mitigation, ethical hackers help organizations proactively address security weaknesses before they can be exploited.

2.   **Compliance:** Vulnerability assessment helps organizations adhere to regulatory requirements and industry standards that mandate regular security assessments.

3.   **Continuous Improvement:** Organizations can use the results of vulnerability assessments to continually improve their security posture, reducing the attack surface and strengthening defenses.

4.   **Incident Prevention:** Addressing vulnerabilities before they are exploited reduces the risk of security incidents and

data breaches.

In conclusion, vulnerability assessment is a pivotal phase in ethical hacking methodology, serving as a proactive measure to uncover and address security weaknesses. Ethical hackers meticulously examine systems and networks, identify vulnerabilities, and provide recommendations for mitigation. This systematic approach not only enhances the security posture of organizations but also empowers them to stay one step ahead of potential adversaries in an ever-evolving digital landscape.

D. Exploitation and Post-Exploitation: The Heart of Ethical Hacking

As ethical hackers venture deeper into their mission to uncover vulnerabilities and secure digital environments, they reach a pivotal juncture—the phases of exploitation and post-exploitation. These phases represent a critical moment in the ethical hacking methodology, where vulnerabilities are leveraged, and control over the target system is established, all with the utmost responsibility and ethical commitment.

Exploitation: Leveraging Vulnerabilities

The exploitation phase involves capitalizing on identified vulnerabilities to gain unauthorized access or control over a target system, network, or application. Ethical hackers use various techniques and strategies to exploit vulnerabilities. Key aspects of exploitation include:

1.   **Proof of Concept (PoC):** Before attempting any exploitation, ethical hackers often develop proof-of-concept exploits to validate the vulnerability's existence and feasibility. This ensures that the identified weakness can indeed be exploited.

2.   **Payload Delivery:** Once a vulnerability is confirmed, ethical hackers design and deliver payloads—malicious code or scripts—that exploit the vulnerability. Payloads can range from simple scripts to more complex pieces of malware.

3.   **Privilege Escalation:** If initial access is limited, ethical hackers may seek ways to escalate their privileges within the target environment. Privilege escalation exploits vulnerabilities that grant higher levels of access, allowing attackers to perform more extensive actions.

4.   **Maintaining Persistence:** To maintain control over the compromised system, ethical hackers often establish backdoors or persistence mechanisms. These mechanisms ensure access even if the system undergoes patching or reboots.

5.   **Exfiltration of Data:** In some cases, ethical hackers may extract data from the compromised system. This data could include sensitive files, passwords, or configuration information.

Post-Exploitation: Consolidating and Securing Control

Post-exploitation is the phase that follows successful exploitation. It involves consolidating and securing control over the compromised system while maintaining discretion and minimizing the risk of detection. Key elements of post-exploitation include:

1.   **Privilege Escalation:** Ethical hackers may continue to seek opportunities for privilege escalation to gain additional control or access within the target environment.

2.   **Lateral Movement:** In more complex environments, ethical hackers may move laterally within the network, seeking to compromise other systems or escalate privileges further.

3.   **Data Collection:** Post-exploitation often involves collecting valuable information from the compromised system. This can include configuration details, user credentials, or sensitive data.

4.   **Maintaining Discretion:** Ethical hackers aim to maintain discretion and avoid actions that could trigger security alarms or raise suspicion. This includes careful monitoring of security logs and avoiding disruptive actions.

5.   **Reporting and Documentation:** Throughout the post-exploitation phase, ethical hackers maintain detailed records of

their actions. These records are crucial for later analysis and reporting to the organization.

Ethical Considerations

In both the exploitation and post-exploitation phases, ethical hackers operate with a strong sense of responsibility and ethical commitment. Key ethical considerations include:

1.   **Authorized Access:** Ethical hackers only exploit vulnerabilities and access systems for which they have explicit authorization. Unauthorized access is strictly prohibited.

2.   **Data Privacy:** Ethical hackers respect the privacy of data and information they encounter during their assessments. They do not engage in data theft or unauthorized disclosure.

3.   **Legal Compliance:** All actions undertaken during ethical hacking engagements must adhere to local, national, and international laws and regulations. Ethical hackers avoid any activities that could lead to legal consequences.

4.   **Transparency:** Ethical hackers maintain open and transparent communication with the organization that has engaged their services. They promptly report findings, vulnerabilities, and actions taken.

The Value of Exploitation and Post-Exploitation

The phases of exploitation and post-exploitation serve essential purposes within ethical hacking methodology:

1.   **Validation of Vulnerabilities:** Exploitation confirms the existence and exploitability of identified vulnerabilities, providing organizations with tangible evidence of weaknesses that need addressing.

2.   **Real-World Impact Assessment:** Successful exploitation demonstrates the potential real-world impact of a vulnerability, emphasizing the urgency of remediation.

3.   **Risk Reduction:** Through the controlled post-exploitation phase, ethical hackers assist organizations in identifying weaknesses in their security controls, enabling the development of more robust defenses.

4.   **Proactive Defense:** Ethical hackers help organizations understand how adversaries might operate in real-world scenarios, allowing them to proactively defend against malicious attackers.

In conclusion, the exploitation and post-exploitation phases represent the heart of ethical hacking, where vulnerabilities are leveraged to gain insight into a target environment and improve security measures. Ethical hackers perform these phases with unwavering ethical commitment, following strict authorization and legal compliance guidelines. Through these phases, organizations can better understand and address their security weaknesses, enhancing their overall cybersecurity posture.

E. Reporting and Documentation: The Ethical Hacker's Compass

In the intricate world of ethical hacking, success isn't just about finding vulnerabilities and securing digital assets; it's equally about conveying findings, insights, and recommendations effectively. The phase of reporting and documentation is where the ethical hacker transforms their discoveries into a comprehensive report—a critical tool that guides organizations toward a more secure future.

The Essence of Reporting and Documentation

Reporting and documentation in ethical hacking is a structured process of recording, analyzing, and presenting the results of security assessments, vulnerability assessments, and penetration tests. This phase involves several key elements:

1.   **Findings Compilation:** Ethical hackers compile a detailed list of vulnerabilities, weaknesses, and security issues identified during the assessment. This includes a thorough description of each finding, its severity, and the potential impact on the organization.

2.   **Risk Assessment:** Each identified vulnerability is assessed for its potential risk and impact. This involves evaluating factors such as the likelihood of exploitation, potential damage, and any associated compliance or regulatory implications.

3.   **Recommendations:** Ethical hackers provide specific and actionable recommendations for addressing each identified vulnerability. Recommendations may include applying patches, configuring security controls, or implementing additional security measures.

4.   **Evidence:** The report includes evidence to support each finding, such as screenshots, log entries, or any artifacts from the assessment process. This evidence helps validate the findings and assists in remediation efforts.

5.   **Executive Summary:** An executive summary provides a high-level overview of the assessment's key findings, risks, and recommendations. This section is often tailored for non-technical stakeholders and executives.

Report Structure and Contents

An effective ethical hacking report typically follows a structured format, including the following key sections:

1.   **Executive Summary:** This section provides a concise summary of the assessment's objectives, key findings, and high-

level recommendations. It is designed for busy executives and decision-makers who need a quick overview.

2.   **Introduction:** The introduction sets the context for the assessment, outlining its scope, objectives, and any limitations. It also provides background information on the organization and its systems.

3.   **Methodology:** Ethical hackers explain the methodology and approach used during the assessment. This section ensures transparency and helps readers understand how the assessment was conducted.

4.   **Findings:** The findings section is the heart of the report, presenting a detailed list of vulnerabilities, weaknesses, and security issues. Each finding is described in depth, including its impact, risk rating, and recommendations for remediation.

5.   **Risk Assessment:** This section provides a more comprehensive analysis of the identified vulnerabilities, including their potential impact on the organization and any associated risks. Risk assessments may use standardized methodologies like CVSS (Common Vulnerability Scoring System).

6.   **Recommendations:** Ethical hackers offer specific and actionable recommendations for addressing each vulnerability. These recommendations are often prioritized based on risk and criticality.

7.   **Appendices:** Appendices include additional information, evidence, or technical details that support the findings and recommendations. This can include screenshots, network diagrams, and log excerpts.

Key Considerations

Reporting and documentation are not just about delivering information; they are also about facilitating action and understanding:

1.   **Clarity and Conciseness:** Reports should be clear and concise, avoiding jargon and technical language when presenting findings to non-technical stakeholders.

2.   **Prioritization:** Vulnerabilities and recommendations should be prioritized based on risk and potential impact to help organizations address the most critical issues first.

3.   **Actionability:** Recommendations should be actionable and realistic, providing organizations with a clear path to remediation.

4.   **Compliance and Regulations:** Ethical hackers should consider any relevant compliance requirements or industry standards in their recommendations.

Value of Reporting and Documentation

The reporting and documentation phase in ethical hacking methodology serves several critical purposes:

1.   **Communication:** It facilitates clear and effective communication between ethical hackers and the organization. Findings, risks, and recommendations are presented in a way that is understandable to technical and non-technical stakeholders.

2.   **Decision Support:** Reports help organizations make informed decisions about prioritizing and addressing vulnerabilities. They provide a roadmap for improving security.

3.   **Transparency:** Reporting demonstrates transparency and ethical conduct, ensuring that organizations understand the full scope of the assessment and its implications.

4.   **Continuous Improvement:** Organizations can use the information in reports to continually enhance their security posture, reducing the likelihood of future security incidents.

In conclusion, the reporting and documentation phase in ethical hacking is not just a formality but a vital component of the process. It transforms technical findings into actionable insights that empower organizations to strengthen their security defenses. Ethical hackers play a crucial role in bridging the gap between technical and non-technical stakeholders, ensuring that security vulnerabilities are understood and addressed effectively.

Chapter 4:

Footprinting and Reconnaissance

Before the first step is taken in the intricate dance of ethical hacking, there lies a crucial prelude—footprinting and reconnaissance. This chapter delves into the art of digital espionage, a meticulous process where ethical hackers don their detective hats to gather intelligence about their target. Just as a skilled detective studies the subtle clues of a crime scene, ethical hackers examine the digital breadcrumbs left across the vast expanse of the internet.

The Digital Detective's Toolkit

Footprinting and reconnaissance are the cornerstones of any successful ethical hacking engagement. They are the means by which ethical hackers uncover the hidden secrets of systems, networks, and individuals. In this chapter, we embark on a journey that explores the techniques, tools, and strategies used to meticulously assemble a digital profile of a target.

From passive reconnaissance methods, such as open-source intelligence (OSINT) gathering and Google Dorking, to the more active and probing phases of port scanning and service enumeration, we unveil the steps taken to map the digital landscape. Each footprint left behind by a system, service, or individual becomes a piece of the puzzle, revealing potential vulnerabilities and pathways into the target.

The Chessboard of Cybersecurity

Much like a chess player surveying the board, ethical hackers analyze the information they gather during this phase to strategize their next moves. Footprinting and reconnaissance provide insights into the target's infrastructure, the technology it employs, and the potential weak points that could be exploited.

But ethical hacking is not a game of chance or a wild chase; it's a calculated dance where each move is deliberate and purposeful. This chapter lays the groundwork for the subsequent phases, setting the stage for ethical hackers to operate with precision, informed by knowledge, and guided by ethical principles.

As we navigate through the intricacies of footprinting and reconnaissance, remember that this phase is not about malicious intent but about fortifying digital defenses. It is a testament to the ethical hacker's commitment to uncover vulnerabilities before adversaries can exploit them, safeguarding the digital realm with vigilance and responsibility.

A. Footprinting Techniques: Tracing Digital Footprints

Footprinting is the foundational phase of reconnaissance in ethical hacking, where the objective is to gather information about a target system, network, or organization. In this phase, ethical hackers employ various techniques to trace and collect digital footprints that provide insight into the target's digital presence and infrastructure.

1. **Open-Source Intelligence (OSINT):** OSINT is a cornerstone of footprinting, involving the collection and analysis of publicly available information from a wide range of sources. Ethical hackers harness the power of search engines, social media, company websites, job postings, news articles, and public records to piece together information about the target. This can include details about employees, technologies in use, recent news, organizational structure, and more.

2. **Google Dorking:** Google Dorking, or Google hacking, utilizes advanced search operators to uncover specific information that may not be readily accessible through standard searches. Ethical hackers craft precise queries to reveal hidden or sensitive data, including file directories, login pages, and potentially vulnerable systems.

3. **Email Harvesting:** Email addresses are valuable pieces of information. Ethical hackers may use tools or techniques

to harvest email addresses associated with the target organization. These addresses can be used for further reconnaissance and social engineering attacks.

4. **WHOIS Lookup:** WHOIS databases contain registration information for internet domains. Ethical hackers use WHOIS lookup tools to retrieve data about domain ownership, registration dates, and contact information. This information helps in understanding the domain landscape of the target.

5. **DNS Enumeration:** DNS enumeration involves querying DNS servers to gather information about domain names and their associated IP addresses. Ethical hackers can identify subdomains, mail servers, and other network infrastructure details through DNS enumeration.

6. **Social Media Analysis:** Organizations often share valuable information on social media platforms. Ethical hackers examine the social media presence of the target, looking for clues about technologies in use, employee profiles, and potential security lapses.

7. **Publicly Available Reports:** Organizations sometimes publish security or vulnerability reports, compliance documents, or whitepapers. Ethical hackers scour these reports for insights into the target's technology stack, security posture, and potential vulnerabilities.

8.   **Job Postings and Employee Profiles:** Job postings can reveal information about technology requirements, while employee profiles on platforms like LinkedIn provide details about the target's workforce, including potential entry points for social engineering attacks.

9.   **Metadata Analysis:** Metadata embedded in files, documents, and images can reveal sensitive information, such as author names, document revisions, and software versions. Ethical hackers examine metadata for hidden insights.

10.   **Competitive Intelligence:** Ethical hackers may analyze competitors' websites, job listings, and public information to gain insights into industry trends, technology choices, and potential vulnerabilities that could apply to the target organization.

Challenges and Considerations

While footprinting is a critical phase, ethical hackers must conduct these activities within legal and ethical boundaries:

1.   **Respect Privacy:** Ethical hackers should be cautious not to intrude into individuals' privacy while gathering information. They should focus on the organization's digital footprint rather than targeting individuals' personal information.

2.   **Authorized Access:** All footprinting activities should be conducted with explicit authorization from the organization or

system owner. Unauthorized access is strictly prohibited.

3. **Legal Compliance:** Ethical hackers must comply with applicable laws and regulations governing data collection and privacy, such as the General Data Protection Regulation (GDPR) in Europe.

4. **Ethical Responsibility:** Ethical hackers should uphold high ethical standards throughout the footprinting process, ensuring that their actions do not cause harm or disruption to the target organization.

In conclusion, footprinting techniques are the first steps in the reconnaissance phase of ethical hacking. They enable ethical hackers to gather valuable information about the target's digital presence and infrastructure. By piecing together these digital footprints, ethical hackers gain critical insights that guide subsequent phases of the ethical hacking process, ultimately leading to a more secure digital environment for organizations.

B. Information Gathering Tools: Peering into the Digital Abyss

In the world of ethical hacking, the reconnaissance phase revolves around collecting valuable information about a target system, network, or organization. To achieve this, ethical hackers rely on a diverse arsenal of information gathering tools, each designed to extract specific details and insights from the vast digital landscape.

These tools, used responsibly and within legal boundaries, enable ethical hackers to paint a comprehensive picture of the target's digital footprint, infrastructure, and potential vulnerabilities. Let's delve into the world of information gathering tools, each serving as a digital detective in the quest for knowledge.

1.   **Nmap (Network Mapper):** Nmap is a versatile and widely used open-source tool for network discovery and vulnerability scanning. Ethical hackers employ Nmap to scan target systems and networks, revealing open ports, services, and operating systems. It's a foundational tool in understanding a target's network landscape.

2.   **Recon-ng:** Recon-ng is a powerful reconnaissance framework designed specifically for information gathering. It integrates with various online resources and APIs, allowing ethical hackers to extract data from social media, search engines, DNS records, and more. It automates the process of collecting OSINT.

3.   **theHarvester:** This tool is ideal for collecting email addresses, subdomains, and virtual hosts associated with a target. Ethical hackers use theHarvester to compile a list of potential entry points and contacts within the organization.

4. **Shodan:** Dubbed the "search engine for the internet of things (IoT)," Shodan specializes in identifying internet-connected devices and services. Ethical hackers leverage Shodan to discover exposed webcams, vulnerable routers, and other IoT devices.

5. **Maltego:** Maltego is a graphical link analysis tool that assists in visualizing data relationships. It's especially useful for mapping the connections between domains, IP addresses, email addresses, and social media profiles to create a comprehensive graph of the target's digital presence.

6. **Metagoofil:** Metagoofil is a metadata gathering tool. It extracts metadata from files, documents, and web pages. This information can reveal sensitive data, such as author names, document revisions, and software versions.

7. **SpiderFoot:** SpiderFoot is an open-source OSINT automation tool that aggregates data from multiple sources to create a holistic profile of the target. It collects information about domains, hosts, IP addresses, email addresses, and more.

8. **FOCA (Fingerprinting Organizations with Collected Archives):** FOCA is designed to extract metadata, hidden documents, and other useful information from documents and web pages. It's particularly valuable for gathering data from corporate documents and websites.

9. **Harvesting Tools:** Various tools specialize in harvesting email addresses, usernames, and subdomains. Examples include theHarvester, FOCA, and EmailHarvester. These tools help ethical hackers compile lists of potential targets or entry points.

10. **Social Media Scrapers:** Custom scripts or tools like Scrapy can be used to scrape social media platforms for information about employees, company culture, and potential security vulnerabilities.

Challenges and Considerations

While information gathering tools are indispensable in the reconnaissance phase, ethical hackers must adhere to strict guidelines to ensure ethical and legal conduct:

1. **Authorized Access:** Ethical hackers must obtain explicit authorization from the target organization or system owner before using information gathering tools.

2. **Legal Compliance:** Information gathering activities should comply with local, national, and international laws and regulations, including data privacy laws.

3. **Respect Privacy:** Ethical hackers should avoid intruding into individuals' privacy while collecting information. Personal information should be handled with care and

responsibility.

4.   **Ethical Responsibility:** High ethical standards must be maintained throughout the information gathering process, ensuring that actions do not cause harm or disruption to the target organization.

In conclusion, information gathering tools are essential components of the ethical hacking toolkit, enabling ethical hackers to uncover valuable insights about target systems, networks, and organizations. These tools empower ethical hackers to assemble a detailed profile of the target's digital presence, laying the foundation for subsequent phases of the ethical hacking process. Ethical conduct, respect for privacy, and adherence to legal boundaries are paramount when utilizing these tools to ensure responsible and effective reconnaissance.

C. Social Engineering: The Art of Human Hacking

In the world of ethical hacking, technical prowess and cybersecurity tools are only part of the equation. Understanding the human element is equally crucial, and that's where social engineering comes into play. Social engineering is the art of manipulating people to divulge confidential information, grant unauthorized access, or perform actions that compromise security. Ethical hackers leverage social engineering techniques to assess an organization's vulnerability to human manipulation and to strengthen its defenses.

The Psychology of Social Engineering

Social engineering exploits human psychology, relying on aspects of trust, authority, curiosity, and urgency to manipulate individuals into taking actions that benefit the attacker. Understanding these psychological triggers is key to effective social engineering:

1.   **Trust:** Attackers often impersonate trusted entities or individuals to gain victims' trust. This could involve posing as IT support, a coworker, or a service provider.

2.   **Authority:** Impersonating someone in a position of authority, such as a manager or a supervisor, can convince victims to comply with requests they might otherwise question.

3.   **Curiosity:** Attackers create scenarios that pique victims' curiosity, prompting them to click on malicious links, open suspicious attachments, or reveal sensitive information to satisfy their curiosity.

4.   **Urgency:** Fabricating emergencies or time-sensitive situations can pressure victims into acting quickly, bypassing their usual skepticism.

Common Social Engineering Techniques

Ethical hackers use various social engineering techniques to test an organization's susceptibility to manipulation:

1.   **Phishing:** Phishing attacks involve sending deceptive emails or messages that appear legitimate, often with links to fake websites or requests for login credentials. These attacks prey on trust and curiosity.

2.   **Pretexting:** Pretexting involves creating a fabricated scenario to obtain information or access. For example, an attacker might impersonate a vendor and request sensitive data from an unsuspecting employee.

3.   **Baiting:** Baiting lures victims with offers or enticing content, such as free software downloads or USB drives. Once the bait is taken, malware is installed or sensitive data is compromised.

4.   **Tailgating (Piggybacking):** Attackers gain physical access to secure areas by following authorized personnel through locked doors or gates without proper authorization.

5.   **Quid Pro Quo:** In a quid pro quo attack, an attacker offers something in exchange for information or access. For instance, they might offer free software in exchange for login credentials.

6.   **Impersonation:** Attackers may impersonate trusted individuals or services, such as tech support, to trick victims into taking specific actions or revealing information.

The Role of Education and Awareness

One of the most effective defenses against social engineering is education and awareness. Organizations invest in training programs to educate employees about the dangers of social engineering and how to recognize and respond to potential threats. Key principles include:

1.   **Recognizing Red Flags:** Employees learn to identify suspicious requests, unsolicited emails, or unusual behavior that might indicate a social engineering attempt.

2.   **Verification Protocols:** Implementing strict verification processes for sensitive actions, such as confirming a request's legitimacy through secondary means.

3.   **Secure Communication:** Encouraging secure communication channels for sensitive information sharing, such as encrypted emails and phone calls.

4.   **Incident Reporting:** Establishing clear procedures for employees to report suspected social engineering attempts.

Ethical Use of Social Engineering

In ethical hacking, the use of social engineering techniques is governed by strict ethical guidelines:

1.   **Authorized Testing:** Social engineering activities must be conducted with explicit authorization from the organization or system owner.

2.   **Consent:** Participants, such as employees, should provide informed consent to be part of social engineering testing. They should also receive proper debriefing after the testing.

3.   **Minimization of Harm:** Ethical hackers should minimize the risk of psychological or emotional harm to individuals involved in testing.

4.   **No Unauthorized Access:** Social engineering should not lead to unauthorized access or disclosure of sensitive data beyond what is necessary for testing purposes.

In conclusion, social engineering is a powerful but inherently risky technique in ethical hacking that exploits human psychology to compromise security. Ethical hackers use it as a tool to assess and reinforce an organization's defenses against such attacks. Understanding the psychological tactics involved and educating employees about social engineering threats are essential components of a robust cybersecurity strategy. Ethical conduct and adherence to ethical guidelines are paramount when employing social engineering techniques in ethical hacking engagements.

D. Footprinting Countermeasures: Defending the Digital Fortress

In the world of ethical hacking, the reconnaissance phase, particularly footprinting, is where attackers gather information to understand a target's vulnerabilities. Organizations must be proactive in their defense, employing a range of countermeasures to thwart these information-gathering efforts and safeguard their digital assets.

1. Access Control and Authorization:

- **User Access Policies:** Implement stringent user access policies that restrict access to sensitive information. Ensure that employees have access only to the data necessary for their roles.

- **Multi-Factor Authentication (MFA):** Enforce MFA for accessing critical systems and applications. This additional layer of security makes it significantly harder for unauthorized users to gain access.

2. Data Classification and Protection:

- **Data Classification:** Classify data based on its

sensitivity. This helps prioritize protection efforts and ensures that highly sensitive information receives the most robust security measures.

- **Encryption:** Encrypt sensitive data both in transit and at rest to protect it from unauthorized access, even if attackers manage to gain access to systems.

3. Social Engineering Awareness:

- **Training and Education:** Conduct regular security awareness training for employees to recognize and resist social engineering attempts, including phishing and pretexting.

- **Incident Reporting:** Establish clear channels for employees to report suspicious activities or potential social engineering attempts promptly.

4. Internet Footprint Reduction:

- **Domain and DNS Management:** Review and control your domain registrations and DNS configurations. Reduce the exposure of sensitive information by minimizing public-facing DNS records.

- **Robot.txt:** Use a robots.txt file to control web crawlers' access to specific parts of your website, limiting the exposure of sensitive information.

5. Online Reputation Management:

- **Monitor Online Presence:** Continuously monitor your organization's online presence, including mentions on social media, forums, and review sites, to detect unauthorized or damaging information.

- **Brand Protection:** Register domain names and social media accounts related to your brand to prevent malicious actors from impersonating your organization.

6. Strong Password Policies:

- **Password Complexity:** Enforce strong password policies that require complex passwords and regular password changes.

- **Password Managers:** Encourage employees to use password managers to create and store strong, unique passwords for each account.

7. Regular Vulnerability Scanning:

- **Network Scanning:** Conduct regular network vulnerability scans to identify and address security weaknesses promptly.

- **Patch Management:** Keep systems and software up to date with the latest security patches to mitigate known vulnerabilities.

8. Network Segmentation:

- **Segmented Networks:** Segment your network to limit lateral movement in case of a breach. This prevents attackers from easily moving from one part of the network to another.

9. Incident Response Plan:

- **IR Team:** Establish an incident response (IR) team with clear roles and responsibilities to respond effectively to any security incidents, including those related to footprinting.

- **Testing:** Regularly test and update the incident response plan to ensure its effectiveness in addressing security incidents.

10. Legal Measures:

- **Terms of Service (ToS):** Include clauses in your organization's ToS that prohibit the use of information gathering techniques or tools without authorization.

- **Digital Millennium Copyright Act (DMCA):** Leverage legal mechanisms like DMCA takedown notices to remove unauthorized or infringing content from the internet.

11. Ethical Hacking Engagements:

- **Penetration Testing:** Conduct regular penetration tests and ethical hacking engagements to identify and address weaknesses proactively.

- **Engage Ethical Hackers:** Employ ethical hackers to assess your organization's security posture from an attacker's perspective, helping you discover and remediate vulnerabilities.

12. Threat Intelligence Sharing:

- **Information Sharing:** Participate in threat intelligence sharing communities and organizations to stay informed about emerging threats and footprinting tactics.

- **Collaboration:** Collaborate with peers and industry partners to share threat information and best practices for mitigating footprinting risks.

13. Privacy Compliance:

- **Data Protection Regulations:** Comply with data protection regulations like GDPR, which mandate stringent data protection measures.

- **Privacy by Design:** Implement privacy by design principles, ensuring that data protection is integrated into all processes and systems.

14. Vendor and Third-Party Assessments:

- **Vendor Security Assessments:** Assess the security practices of third-party vendors and partners to ensure they adhere to robust security standards, minimizing the risk of exposure through third-party relationships.

In conclusion, organizations must adopt a multi-faceted approach to defend against footprinting activities in the reconnaissance phase of ethical hacking. By combining technical measures, user education, legal safeguards, and proactive security practices, organizations can significantly reduce their vulnerability to information gathering techniques and enhance their overall cybersecurity posture. A vigilant and well-prepared organization is more likely to deter attackers and protect sensitive data.

Chapter 5:

Network Scanning

In the intricate world of ethical hacking, where security is paramount, the ability to see beyond the surface is a coveted skill. Network scanning is the lens through which ethical hackers peer into the digital landscape, unveiling the hidden architecture of systems and networks. It's a phase that goes beyond the visible, mapping the vast expanse of networked devices and services with precision.

Unveiling the Digital Terrain

Network scanning is the art of systematically probing computer networks to discover open ports, services, and vulnerabilities. In this chapter, we embark on a journey that explores the tools, techniques, and strategies used to reveal the digital terrain. Just as cartographers map uncharted lands, ethical hackers chart the course of network packets, uncovering potential gateways and weaknesses.

From the subtleties of network mapping to the intricacies of port scanning and vulnerability detection, we dive deep into the methodologies that enable ethical hackers to navigate the digital labyrinth. With each scan, a layer of the network's secrets is unveiled, providing insights that guide security enhancements and fortify digital defenses.

The Guardians of Cyberspace

In an era where networked systems underpin every facet of modern life, ethical hackers stand as the guardians of cyberspace. They wield network scanning tools not to exploit but to protect, not to disrupt but to fortify. With each scan, they identify potential vulnerabilities before adversaries can exploit them, ensuring that organizations remain resilient in the face of evolving threats.

As we venture into the realm of network scanning, remember that this phase is not a quest for vulnerabilities alone; it's a pursuit of knowledge and security. It's an embodiment of the ethical hacker's commitment to safeguarding digital realms, one scan at a time.

A. Network Mapping: Charting the Digital Landscape

In the realm of ethical hacking, understanding the terrain is paramount. Network mapping is the crucial first step, akin to a cartographer surveying uncharted lands, enabling ethical hackers to chart the digital landscape of systems and networks. It is the process of discovering and documenting the structure, layout, and interconnectedness of devices and services within a network.

The Significance of Network Mapping

Network mapping serves as the foundational pillar of network reconnaissance in ethical hacking. Its primary objectives are:

1.   **Discovery:** Uncover all devices, hosts, and assets within the network. This includes computers, servers, routers, switches, firewalls, and any other networked equipment.

2.   **Visualization:** Create a visual representation of the network's architecture, helping ethical hackers and network administrators understand its layout and relationships.

3.   **Identification:** Identify open ports, services, and protocols running on each discovered device. This information is crucial for assessing potential vulnerabilities.

4.   **Documentation:** Document the findings for reference, analysis, and as a basis for further ethical hacking activities.

Network Mapping Techniques

Ethical hackers employ various techniques and tools for network mapping, each with its strengths and limitations:

1.   **Ping Scanning:** Ping scans use Internet Control Message Protocol (ICMP) requests to determine if a device is online and responsive. Tools like 'ping' or 'fping' are commonly used for this purpose.

2.   **ARP Scanning:** Address Resolution Protocol (ARP) scans reveal the mapping between IP addresses and MAC (Media Access Control) addresses on a local network segment.

3.   **TCP/IP Stack Fingerprinting:** This technique involves sending packets to a target system and analyzing the responses to determine the underlying operating system and version.

4.   **DNS Enumeration:** DNS (Domain Name System) enumeration uncovers hostnames, domain names, and IP addresses associated with a network. Tools like 'nslookup' and 'dig' are used for DNS enumeration.

5.   **SNMP Enumeration:** Simple Network Management Protocol (SNMP) enumeration collects information about network devices and services, including device names, descriptions, and configurations.

6.   **Banner Grabbing:** Banner grabbing involves connecting to open ports and capturing the banner or information displayed by the service running on that port. This helps identify the service and its version.

7.   **NetBIOS Enumeration:** NetBIOS scans reveal Windows-based network shares and resources. Tools like 'nbtscan' and 'enum4linux' are commonly used.

Network Mapping Best Practices

When conducting network mapping in ethical hacking engagements, it's essential to follow best practices to ensure responsible and ethical conduct:

1.   **Authorization:** Obtain explicit authorization from the organization or system owner before performing network mapping activities. Unauthorized scanning is illegal and unethical.

2.   **Minimize Disruption:** Use scanning techniques and tools that minimize disruption to the network. Avoid aggressive or intrusive scans that could impact network performance.

3.   **Documentation:** Carefully document all findings, including IP addresses, hostnames, open ports, and services. This documentation forms the basis for subsequent ethical hacking activities.

4.   **Verify Results:** Cross-verify network mapping results using multiple techniques and tools to ensure accuracy and completeness.

5.   **Respect Privacy:** Avoid scanning systems or devices that may contain sensitive or private information, and do not attempt to access unauthorized data.

Conclusion

In the ethical hacking landscape, network mapping is the compass that guides the journey. It transforms the unknown into the known, allowing ethical hackers to navigate the digital terrain with precision. Armed with insights gained from network mapping, ethical hackers can identify potential vulnerabilities and weaknesses, providing organizations with the knowledge needed to fortify their defenses against cyber threats. Ethical conduct, adherence to legal and ethical guidelines, and responsible mapping practices are fundamental to the success of this crucial reconnaissance phase.

B. Port Scanning Techniques: Uncovering Pathways and Weaknesses

In the intricate dance of ethical hacking, where security hinges on comprehensive knowledge, port scanning takes center stage. It's the process of probing a network or system to uncover open ports, services, and potential vulnerabilities. Port scanning techniques serve as the key to unlocking the digital doors and pathways within a network, allowing ethical hackers to assess its security posture.

The Importance of Port Scanning

Port scanning plays a pivotal role in ethical hacking for several reasons:

1.   **Identification:** Port scanning reveals the ports and services available on a target system or network, enabling ethical hackers to identify potential entry points.

2.   **Enumeration:** It assists in the enumeration of running services, their versions, and configurations. This information is critical for assessing vulnerabilities.

3.   **Security Assessment:** Port scanning allows ethical hackers to assess the security posture of a network by identifying open ports and services that may be targets for exploitation.

4.   **Access Control:** Organizations use port scanning to monitor and enforce access control policies. Unauthorized open ports can indicate security policy violations.

Common Port Scanning Techniques

Ethical hackers employ various port scanning techniques to gain insights into the target's network. Each technique has its advantages and is chosen based on the specific goals of the ethical hacking engagement:

1.   **TCP Connect Scan:** This is the most straightforward port scanning technique. It attempts to establish a full TCP connection with each target port. Successful connections indicate open ports, while unsuccessful attempts signal closed or filtered

ports. The drawback is that it generates extensive logs and is easily detectable.

2. **TCP SYN (Half-Open) Scan:** This scan sends a TCP SYN packet to the target port. If the port is open, the target responds with a SYN-ACK packet, indicating its availability. If the port is closed, the target responds with a RST packet. This scan is stealthier than a TCP Connect Scan and is often used for reconnaissance.

3. **TCP NULL, FIN, and Xmas Scans:** These scans send various combinations of TCP NULL, FIN, and URG flags in the packet header. Open ports respond differently to these flags. While these scans are stealthy, they may not work against all target systems.

4. **UDP Scan:** UDP (User Datagram Protocol) scans probe UDP ports to identify open services. Since UDP is connectionless and stateless, this scan relies on target responses or lack thereof. It can be slow and unreliable but is essential for identifying UDP-based services.

5. **ACK Scan:** This scan sends TCP ACK (Acknowledgment) packets to target ports. It aims to determine if a port is filtered by a firewall. If the firewall allows traffic through but blocks unsolicited ACK packets, the port is considered open. Otherwise, it's filtered or closed.

6.   **Idle Scan (Zombie Scan):** This advanced scan uses a third-party host (the "zombie") to scan the target without revealing the true source. By exploiting differences in how TCP/IP stacks handle certain conditions, it can be challenging to detect.

Port Scanning Best Practices

Ethical hackers must adhere to best practices to conduct responsible and ethical port scanning:

1.   **Authorization:** Obtain explicit authorization from the organization or system owner before performing port scanning activities. Unauthorized scanning is illegal and unethical.

2.   **Minimize Disruption:** Use scanning techniques and tools that minimize network disruption. Avoid aggressive scans that could impact network performance.

3.   **Documentation:** Carefully document scan results, including open ports, services, and any potential vulnerabilities discovered. This documentation is crucial for subsequent ethical hacking activities.

4.   **Verify Results:** Cross-verify scan results using multiple techniques and tools to ensure accuracy and completeness.

5.   **Respect Privacy:** Avoid scanning systems or devices that may contain sensitive or private information, and do not

attempt to access unauthorized data.

Conclusion

Port scanning techniques are the key to uncovering the pathways and weaknesses within a network, enabling ethical hackers to assess its security posture. Armed with knowledge gained from port scanning, ethical hackers can identify potential vulnerabilities, assess the target's security, and recommend measures to fortify its defenses. Responsible and ethical conduct, adherence to legal and ethical guidelines, and skillful application of port scanning techniques are paramount in the successful execution of this essential reconnaissance phase of ethical hacking.

C. Vulnerability Scanning: Safeguarding the Digital Bastions

In the ever-evolving landscape of cybersecurity, ethical hackers play a critical role in identifying and mitigating vulnerabilities that threaten the integrity of systems and networks. Vulnerability scanning stands as a pivotal technique within their arsenal, allowing them to proactively search for weaknesses, misconfigurations, and potential entry points that malicious actors might exploit.

The Significance of Vulnerability Scanning

Vulnerability scanning serves as the linchpin of a robust cybersecurity strategy, delivering several crucial benefits:

1.   **Risk Assessment:** It provides a comprehensive view of an organization's security posture by identifying vulnerabilities and their potential impact on the network and systems.

2.   **Prioritization:** By ranking vulnerabilities based on severity, ethical hackers help organizations prioritize remediation efforts, ensuring that critical vulnerabilities are addressed first.

3.   **Compliance:** Vulnerability scanning aids in compliance with industry regulations and standards that require organizations to maintain a secure infrastructure.

4.   **Continuous Monitoring:** Regular scanning helps organizations monitor the effectiveness of security measures and track improvements over time.

Types of Vulnerability Scanning

Ethical hackers use various types of vulnerability scanning techniques, each tailored to specific objectives:

1.   **Network Vulnerability Scanning:** This type of scanning focuses on identifying vulnerabilities within the network infrastructure, such as misconfigured routers, unpatched services,

or weak passwords.

2.   **Web Application Scanning:** Web application scanning is designed to uncover vulnerabilities in web applications, including SQL injection, cross-site scripting (XSS), and security misconfigurations.

3.   **Host-Based Scanning:** Host-based scanning assesses the vulnerabilities present on individual hosts or devices, such as servers and workstations, by analyzing their configurations and installed software.

4.   **Authenticated Scanning:** Authenticated scanning requires valid credentials to assess vulnerabilities within systems accurately. It provides a more thorough examination of host-based vulnerabilities.

5.   **Unauthenticated Scanning:** Unauthenticated scanning does not require credentials and is used to identify vulnerabilities that can be detected without direct access to the target system.

Vulnerability Scanning Tools

Ethical hackers rely on a range of specialized tools for conducting vulnerability scanning. Some popular examples include:

1.   **Nessus:** Nessus is a widely used vulnerability scanning

tool known for its extensive vulnerability database and broad platform support. It can perform both authenticated and unauthenticated scans.

2.   **OpenVAS:** OpenVAS is an open-source vulnerability assessment system that offers scanning capabilities for network, web applications, and hosts. It includes a comprehensive database of known vulnerabilities.

3.   **Qualys:** Qualys provides cloud-based vulnerability management and scanning services. It offers scalability, real-time reporting, and integration with other security tools.

4.   **Nexpose:** Nexpose, by Rapid7, is a vulnerability management solution that combines vulnerability scanning with risk assessment and reporting. It provides detailed remediation recommendations.

5.   **Burp Suite:** Burp Suite is a web application security scanner used for identifying web vulnerabilities like SQL injection and XSS. It also includes a proxy and other tools for web application testing.

Vulnerability Scanning Best Practices

To conduct effective and responsible vulnerability scanning, ethical hackers adhere to several best practices:

1.   **Authorization:** Obtain explicit authorization from the

organization or system owner before conducting vulnerability scanning activities. Unauthorized scanning can disrupt systems and networks and may be illegal.

2.   **Minimize Disruption:** Use scanning techniques and tools that minimize disruption to the network and systems. Avoid aggressive scans that could impact network performance.

3.   **Documentation:** Thoroughly document scan results, including identified vulnerabilities, their severity, and potential impact. This documentation forms the basis for remediation efforts.

4.   **Regular Scanning:** Perform vulnerability scanning regularly to ensure that new vulnerabilities are promptly identified and addressed. Scanning should be part of an ongoing security program.

5.   **Remediation:** Work closely with the organization to prioritize and remediate identified vulnerabilities. Provide recommendations for mitigating risks effectively.

Conclusion

Vulnerability scanning is the beacon that illuminates the dark corners of systems and networks, enabling ethical hackers to identify and address potential vulnerabilities. Armed with the knowledge gained from vulnerability scanning, ethical hackers help organizations fortify their defenses, mitigate risks, and maintain a strong security posture. Responsible and ethical conduct, adherence to legal and ethical guidelines, and expert utilization of vulnerability scanning tools are essential in the successful execution of this critical reconnaissance phase of ethical hacking.

D. Scanning Tools and Utilities: The Eyes and Ears of Ethical Hackers

In the complex arena of ethical hacking, where the boundary between security and vulnerability is razor-thin, scanning tools and utilities act as the eyes and ears of ethical hackers. These specialized software applications are the instruments through which ethical hackers gain insights into networks, systems, and applications, allowing them to uncover vulnerabilities, assess security postures, and fortify digital defenses.

The Crucial Role of Scanning Tools

Scanning tools are indispensable in ethical hacking for several compelling reasons:

1.   **Efficiency:** Scanning tools automate the process of probing networks and systems for vulnerabilities, significantly reducing the time and effort required for manual inspection.

2.   **Comprehensiveness:**   These   tools   perform

comprehensive assessments, examining a wide range of potential vulnerabilities, including open ports, misconfigurations, and security weaknesses.

3.   **Accuracy:** Scanning tools provide precise and consistent results, minimizing the risk of human error inherent in manual assessments.

4.   **Documentation:** They generate detailed reports that document scan results, making it easier for ethical hackers to communicate findings and recommendations to organizations.

Types of Scanning Tools and Utilities

Ethical hackers employ a variety of scanning tools and utilities tailored to different aspects of their assessments:

1.   **Port Scanners:** Port scanning tools, such as Nmap and Masscan, are designed to discover open ports on target systems, identify services running on those ports, and assess potential vulnerabilities associated with those services.

2.   **Vulnerability Scanners:** Vulnerability scanning tools, like Nessus and OpenVAS, focus on identifying weaknesses within systems and networks. They analyze configurations, software versions, and known vulnerabilities to generate reports of potential security issues.

3.   **Network Mapping Tools:** Network mapping tools,

including Zenmap (Nmap's graphical frontend) and Netcat, assist in creating visual representations of network architectures, helping ethical hackers understand the layout and relationships between devices.

4. **Web Application Scanners:** Web application scanners like Burp Suite and OWASP ZAP are specialized tools for identifying vulnerabilities in web applications, such as SQL injection, cross-site scripting (XSS), and security misconfigurations.

5. **Password Cracking Tools:** Password cracking utilities like John the Ripper and Hashcat are used to test the strength of passwords and assess the risk of unauthorized access.

6. **Packet Sniffers:** Packet sniffers like Wireshark capture and analyze network traffic, allowing ethical hackers to inspect data packets and discover potential security issues.

7. **Banner Grabbers:** Banner grabbing tools, such as Banner and WhatWeb, extract information about services running on open ports by analyzing the banners or responses provided by those services.

8. **DNS Enumeration Tools:** DNS enumeration utilities like Dig and Fierce assist in gathering information about a target's DNS infrastructure, including hostnames, IP addresses, and name servers.

Selecting the Right Tool for the Job

Ethical hackers select scanning tools based on the specific objectives of their assessments, the type of target (network, system, web application, etc.), and the scope of the engagement. Choosing the right tool ensures that the assessment is thorough, efficient, and aligned with the organization's goals.

Scanning Best Practices

To conduct responsible and ethical scanning activities, ethical hackers follow best practices:

1.   **Authorization:** Obtain explicit authorization from the organization or system owner before using scanning tools. Unauthorized scanning can disrupt systems and networks and may be illegal.

2.   **Minimize Disruption:** Use scanning techniques and tools that minimize disruption to the network and systems. Avoid aggressive scans that could impact network performance.

3.   **Documentation:** Thoroughly document scan results, including identified vulnerabilities, their severity, and potential impact. This documentation serves as the basis for remediation efforts.

4.   **Remediation:** Work closely with the organization to prioritize and remediate identified vulnerabilities. Provide

recommendations for mitigating risks effectively.

Conclusion

Scanning tools and utilities are the invaluable instruments through which ethical hackers dissect networks, systems, and applications. Armed with these tools, ethical hackers uncover vulnerabilities, assess security postures, and collaborate with organizations to fortify their digital defenses. Responsible and ethical conduct, adherence to legal and ethical guidelines, and expert utilization of scanning tools are fundamental in the successful execution of ethical hacking assessments, ensuring the safeguarding of digital realms against evolving cyber threats.

Chapter 6:

Enumeration and Exploitation

In the intricate art of ethical hacking, there comes a point when knowledge transforms into power. Enumeration and exploitation represent the crossroads where that power is harnessed for a higher purpose. These phases mark the transition from identifying potential weaknesses to actively leveraging them, all with the goal of enhancing cybersecurity.

Unveiling the Hidden Details

Enumeration is the art of extracting intricate details about a target network or system, delving beyond the surface to uncover the inner workings and configurations. It's the process of gaining a deeper understanding of the digital landscape, knowing its strengths and vulnerabilities. Once this knowledge is in hand, ethical hackers can tread carefully but decisively into the realm of exploitation.

The Delicate Balance of Power

Enumeration and exploitation are perhaps the most delicate phases of ethical hacking. They require a profound grasp of technology, a commitment to ethics, and a keen sense of responsibility. In these chapters, we embark on a journey that explores the methods, tools, and strategies that ethical hackers use to navigate this terrain.

We will delve into the intricacies of service enumeration, operating system fingerprinting, and the exploitation of vulnerabilities. But always remember that this knowledge is a double-edged sword. It can be a force for protection, illuminating the path to a safer digital world, or a weapon in the wrong hands, causing harm and disruption.

Guardians of the Digital Realm

As we venture deeper into the realms of enumeration and exploitation, remember that ethical hackers are not adversaries but guardians. They are the vigilant watchmen of cyberspace, using their skills to identify vulnerabilities and strengthen digital bastions. Their mission is not to disrupt but to protect, not to exploit but to fortify.

Enumeration and exploitation are the gateways to a deeper understanding of systems and networks. They are tools in the hands of those committed to cybersecurity, paving the way for a safer and more resilient digital future.

A. Service Enumeration: Unveiling the Digital Heartbeat

In the realm of ethical hacking, where the preservation of digital sanctity is paramount, service enumeration plays a pivotal role. It is the phase where ethical hackers peel back the layers of a target system or network, much like a surgeon exploring the intricacies of a beating heart. Service enumeration unveils the critical services, applications, and functionalities that lie beneath the surface, allowing ethical hackers to understand, assess, and potentially exploit them.

The Significance of Service Enumeration

Service enumeration serves as a crucial reconnaissance step in ethical hacking for several compelling reasons:

1.   **Identification:** It identifies and catalogs the services and applications running on target systems. This knowledge provides insights into the attack surface and potential entry points for exploitation.

2.   **Enumeration:** Service enumeration goes beyond identification; it involves collecting detailed information about each service, such as version numbers, configurations, and available functionalities. This information is vital for assessing vulnerabilities.

3.   **Attack Surface Analysis:** Ethical hackers use service

enumeration to map the attack surface, helping them identify potential weaknesses and misconfigurations in the target system.

4.   **Vulnerability Assessment:** Armed with detailed information about services and applications, ethical hackers can conduct vulnerability assessments to determine whether known vulnerabilities exist and can be exploited.

Methods of Service Enumeration

Ethical hackers employ various methods and techniques for service enumeration, each tailored to specific objectives and scenarios:

1.   **Banner Grabbing:** Banner grabbing is the practice of connecting to open ports and capturing the banners or responses provided by the services running on those ports. These banners often reveal information about the service type and version.

2.   **Port Scanning:** Port scanning techniques, such as TCP and UDP scans, are used to identify open ports on a target system. Once open ports are identified, ethical hackers can proceed to enumerate the services running on those ports.

3.   **Network Service Scanning:** This method involves sending crafted packets or queries to network services and analyzing their responses. For example, querying DNS servers for zone transfers or sending SNMP requests to gather information

about network devices.

4.   **Application   Fingerprinting:**   Application fingerprinting techniques identify specific applications or software running on a system based on their unique characteristics, such as responses to specific requests or patterns in network traffic.

5.   **Operating System Fingerprinting:** Sometimes, service enumeration includes determining the underlying operating system of a target system. This information can be useful for tailoring subsequent attacks or exploits.

Tools for Service Enumeration

Ethical hackers have a wide range of tools at their disposal to facilitate service enumeration:

1.   **Nmap:** Nmap (Network Mapper) is a versatile and widely used open-source tool that offers comprehensive port scanning and service enumeration capabilities.

2.   **Banner:** Banner is a simple command-line tool for banner grabbing. It connects to a given IP address and port and retrieves the banner or response from the service running on that port.

3.   **SNMP Enumeration Tools:** Tools like SNMPwalk and snmp-check assist in enumerating network devices and

services through SNMP queries.

4. **DNS Enumeration Tools:** Tools like Dig, NSLookup, and DNSRecon help gather information about DNS servers and their configurations.

5. **Operating System Fingerprinting Tools:** Tools like p0f and Xprobe2 are used to determine the underlying operating system based on network responses.

Service Enumeration Best Practices

To conduct responsible and ethical service enumeration, ethical hackers adhere to best practices:

1. **Authorization:** Obtain explicit authorization from the organization or system owner before conducting service enumeration activities. Unauthorized enumeration can disrupt systems and networks and may be illegal.

2. **Minimize Disruption:** Use enumeration techniques and tools that minimize disruption to the target systems. Avoid aggressive scans that could impact network performance.

3. **Documentation:** Thoroughly document the results of service enumeration, including service types, versions, and any potential vulnerabilities identified. This documentation serves as the foundation for subsequent ethical hacking activities.

4.   **Remediation:** Collaborate with the organization to prioritize and remediate identified vulnerabilities. Provide recommendations for mitigating risks effectively.

Conclusion

Service enumeration is the gateway to understanding the digital heartbeat of a target system or network. Armed with knowledge gained through enumeration, ethical hackers can assess vulnerabilities, strengthen security postures, and fortify digital defenses. Responsible and ethical conduct, adherence to legal and ethical guidelines, and expert utilization of service enumeration techniques and tools are essential for success in this critical reconnaissance phase of ethical hacking, ensuring the protection of digital realms against evolving cyber threats.

B. OS Fingerprinting: Unmasking the Digital Identity

In the intricate world of ethical hacking, where precision and knowledge are paramount, Operating System (OS) fingerprinting stands as a critical reconnaissance technique. It is the art of unveiling the digital identity of a target system, much like a detective identifying a suspect by examining their unique characteristics. OS fingerprinting enables ethical hackers to determine the underlying operating system of a target, offering valuable insights for potential exploits and security assessments.

The Significance of OS Fingerprinting

OS fingerprinting holds immense significance in ethical hacking for several compelling reasons:

1.   **Exploit Tailoring:** Knowledge of the target's operating system is crucial for selecting and tailoring exploits that are most likely to succeed. Different operating systems have distinct vulnerabilities and behaviors.

2.   **Security Assessment:** Understanding the target's operating system helps ethical hackers assess its security posture, vulnerabilities, and patch levels. This information informs risk assessments and potential attack vectors.

3.   **Network Enumeration:** OS fingerprinting is often part of broader network enumeration efforts. It provides valuable data that contributes to the comprehensive mapping of target systems and networks.

Methods of OS Fingerprinting

Ethical hackers employ various methods and techniques for OS fingerprinting, each with its advantages and limitations:

1.   **Active Fingerprinting:** Active OS fingerprinting involves sending specially crafted packets to the target system and analyzing its responses. The characteristics of the responses can reveal the underlying operating system. Tools like Nmap and

Xprobe2 use this method.

2.   **Passive Fingerprinting:** Passive OS fingerprinting relies on observing network traffic between the target system and other devices. By analyzing patterns and behaviors in network packets, ethical hackers can make educated guesses about the target's OS. Tools like p0f are used for passive OS fingerprinting.

3.   **Banner Grabbing:** Banner grabbing, a form of passive fingerprinting, involves connecting to open ports on a target system and capturing the banners or responses from services running on those ports. These banners may contain clues about the operating system.

4.   **Time-to-Live (TTL) Analysis:** TTL analysis involves examining the Time-to-Live value in IP packets as they traverse the network. Different operating systems set TTL values differently, providing hints about the OS type.

5.   **Fragmentation Analysis:** Some operating systems handle packet fragmentation in distinct ways. Ethical hackers can analyze how a target system reassembles fragmented packets to make educated guesses about its OS.

Tools for OS Fingerprinting

Ethical hackers have access to various tools and utilities to facilitate OS fingerprinting:

1.   **Nmap:** Nmap (Network Mapper) is a versatile and widely used open-source tool that offers comprehensive OS fingerprinting capabilities. It uses a combination of active and passive techniques.

2.   **Xprobe2:** Xprobe2 is a specialized tool for active OS fingerprinting. It sends crafted packets to the target and analyzes the responses to determine the operating system.

3.   **p0f:** p0f is a passive OS fingerprinting tool that analyzes network traffic to identify the OS of devices communicating on the network.

4.   **Wireshark:** Wireshark is a packet analysis tool that can be used for passive OS fingerprinting by examining network traffic and identifying patterns associated with specific operating systems.

OS Fingerprinting Best Practices

To conduct responsible and ethical OS fingerprinting, ethical hackers follow best practices:

1.   **Authorization:** Obtain explicit authorization from the organization or system owner before conducting OS fingerprinting activities. Unauthorized fingerprinting can disrupt systems and networks and may be illegal.

2.   **Minimize Disruption:** Use OS fingerprinting

techniques and tools that minimize disruption to the target system. Avoid aggressive scans that could trigger security alarms or impact system performance.

3. **Documentation:** Thoroughly document OS fingerprinting results, including the identified operating system and any supporting evidence. This documentation serves as a foundation for further ethical hacking activities.

4. **Ethical Use:** Ethical hackers must use OS fingerprinting techniques solely for the purpose of security assessments, vulnerability testing, and strengthening the target's security posture.

Conclusion

OS fingerprinting is the art of unmasking the digital identity of a target system, providing ethical hackers with crucial insights into potential vulnerabilities and attack vectors. Armed with knowledge gained through OS fingerprinting, ethical hackers can tailor their approaches, assess security postures, and make informed decisions in their quest to safeguard digital realms against evolving cyber threats. Responsible and ethical conduct, adherence to legal and ethical guidelines, and expert utilization of OS fingerprinting techniques and tools are paramount in the successful execution of this critical reconnaissance phase of ethical hacking.

C. Exploiting Vulnerabilities: Navigating the Gray Area of Ethical Hacking

In the intricate landscape of ethical hacking, where the line between security assessment and potential harm is razor-thin, the phase of exploiting vulnerabilities emerges as both a critical skill and a moral challenge. It is the stage where ethical hackers actively leverage identified weaknesses within a target system or network to test security, uncover critical flaws, and provide recommendations for mitigation.

The Complex Significance of Exploiting Vulnerabilities

Exploiting vulnerabilities in ethical hacking holds multifaceted significance:

1. **Validation of Risk:** Ethical hackers exploit vulnerabilities to validate their existence and assess their potential impact. This step is vital in determining whether a vulnerability is theoretical or represents a real threat.

2. **Proof of Concept:** Demonstrating the exploitation of a vulnerability with a "proof of concept" (PoC) illustrates the tangible risks to stakeholders, facilitating informed decision-making for remediation.

3. **Security Posture Evaluation:** Ethical hackers utilize exploitation as a means to evaluate an organization's overall security posture and identify potential weaknesses that could be

targeted by malicious actors.

4.   **Enhancing Resilience:** By exploiting vulnerabilities and highlighting security gaps, ethical hackers enable organizations to take proactive measures, patch vulnerabilities, and fortify defenses against potential threats.

Methods of Exploiting Vulnerabilities

Ethical hackers employ a variety of methods and techniques for exploiting vulnerabilities, always with the goal of improving security:

1.   **Manual Exploitation:** This approach involves manually crafting and executing exploits to take advantage of identified vulnerabilities. Manual exploitation provides fine-grained control but requires advanced technical expertise.

2.   **Automated Exploitation Tools:** Ethical hackers often use automated tools like Metasploit, Core Impact, and Canvas to streamline and simplify the exploitation process. These tools contain a vast library of pre-built exploits and payloads.

3.   **Privilege Escalation:** After gaining initial access, ethical hackers may escalate their privileges within a system to gain deeper control. This might involve exploiting privilege escalation vulnerabilities or weaknesses in access control mechanisms.

4.   **Client-Side Exploitation:** Client-side exploitation focuses on vulnerabilities in applications or services running on the user's device, such as web browsers or email clients. Malicious content is delivered to exploit these vulnerabilities when the user interacts with it.

5.   **Lateral Movement:** Ethical hackers may exploit one system or user account to pivot and move laterally within a network. This involves finding and exploiting vulnerabilities in other systems to expand their control.

6.   **Social Engineering:** Human vulnerabilities can be just as exploitable as technical ones. Ethical hackers use social engineering tactics to manipulate individuals into divulging sensitive information or taking actions that compromise security.

Ethical Considerations in Exploitation

Exploiting vulnerabilities is a morally and legally complex aspect of ethical hacking. To ensure ethical conduct:

1.   **Authorization:** Ethical hackers must have explicit authorization from the organization or system owner to exploit vulnerabilities. Unauthorized exploitation is illegal and unethical.

2.   **Documentation:** All exploitation activities and results must be meticulously documented to provide transparency, accountability, and the foundation for remediation.

3. **Minimize Harm:** Ethical hackers should aim to minimize disruption and damage while exploiting vulnerabilities. The goal is to demonstrate the existence of risks without causing undue harm.

4. **Responsible Disclosure:** Ethical hackers have an ethical responsibility to report identified vulnerabilities to the organization or vendor responsibly. This allows for timely remediation and protects potential victims.

5. **Benefit Assessment:** Ethical hackers must weigh the potential benefits of exploitation (identifying and mitigating risks) against the potential harm (disruption, data exposure) before proceeding.

Conclusion

Exploiting vulnerabilities is a complex dance in ethical hacking, where knowledge, skill, and ethics converge. Ethical hackers utilize this phase not as an end but as a means to uncover, assess, and ultimately improve the security of digital systems and networks. Responsible and ethical conduct, adherence to legal and ethical guidelines, and expert utilization of exploitation techniques and tools are paramount in the successful execution of this critical phase of ethical hacking. The ultimate aim is to fortify digital realms against evolving cyber threats while respecting the boundaries of ethical and legal standards.

D. Post-Exploitation Techniques: The Art of Pivoting and Control

In the intricate world of ethical hacking, where security breaches can serve as both a test and an opportunity, post-exploitation techniques emerge as a pivotal phase. It represents the stage where ethical hackers, having successfully penetrated a target system or network, navigate the complex terrain of persistence, privilege escalation, data exfiltration, and maintaining control over the compromised environment.

The Multifaceted Significance of Post-Exploitation

Post-exploitation techniques hold multifaceted significance in ethical hacking:

1. **Maintaining Control:** After gaining initial access, ethical hackers use post-exploitation techniques to ensure continued control over the compromised system or network. This control allows for deeper exploration and assessment.

2. **Privilege Escalation:** Ethical hackers seek to escalate privileges to gain higher levels of access within the compromised environment. Privilege escalation can lead to more extensive exploration and data retrieval.

3. **Data Exfiltration:** Post-exploitation techniques enable ethical hackers to exfiltrate valuable information from the compromised environment. This data may include sensitive files,

credentials, or configuration details.

4.   **Pivoting:** Pivoting involves leveraging the compromised system as a gateway to access other systems or networks within the target organization. It allows ethical hackers to expand their influence and assess the broader attack surface.

Methods of Post-Exploitation Techniques

Ethical hackers employ various methods and techniques for post-exploitation, each tailored to the objectives of their assessment:

1.   **Persistence:** Achieving persistence involves ensuring that the hacker's access to the compromised system persists across reboots and system changes. This may involve installing backdoors, rootkits, or creating scheduled tasks.

2.   **Privilege Escalation:** Ethical hackers seek to elevate their privileges within the system or network. This may involve exploiting additional vulnerabilities or misconfigurations to gain administrative or root access.

3.   **Data Exfiltration:** Data exfiltration techniques range from copying files to remote servers to extracting sensitive information through covert channels. Techniques like steganography may be used to hide data within seemingly innocuous files.

4.   **Lateral Movement:** After compromising one system, ethical hackers may pivot to other systems or networks within the organization. This involves exploiting vulnerabilities or weak access controls on additional targets.

5.   **Maintaining Stealth:** Ethical hackers often use anti-forensics and rootkit techniques to hide their presence on the compromised system and evade detection by security monitoring tools.

6.   **Covering Tracks:** Ethical hackers take steps to erase or alter logs, audit trails, and other evidence of their activities to maintain stealth and make detection more challenging.

Tools and Frameworks for Post-Exploitation

Ethical hackers have access to a range of tools and frameworks designed to facilitate post-exploitation activities:

1.   **Metasploit:** Metasploit is a popular and versatile exploitation framework that includes post-exploitation modules for maintaining control, escalating privileges, and exfiltrating data.

2.   **PowerShell Empire:** PowerShell Empire is a post-exploitation framework that leverages PowerShell for advanced persistence, privilege escalation, and data exfiltration.

3.   **Cobalt Strike:** Cobalt Strike is a commercial post-

exploitation tool that provides advanced features for maintaining control, lateral movement, and exfiltration.

4.   **Beacon:** Beacon is a lightweight and versatile post-exploitation tool included in Cobalt Strike. It offers stealthy communication and control features.

Ethical Considerations in Post-Exploitation

Post-exploitation activities in ethical hacking must adhere to strict ethical guidelines:

1.   **Authorization:** Ethical hackers must have explicit authorization from the organization or system owner to engage in post-exploitation activities. Unauthorized actions are illegal and unethical.

2.   **Responsible Conduct:** Ethical hackers should conduct post-exploitation activities responsibly, aiming to minimize disruption and harm while maximizing the identification and remediation of security vulnerabilities.

3.   **Documentation:** Ethical hackers must document all post-exploitation activities, including findings, actions taken, and recommendations. This documentation provides transparency and supports the organization's efforts to improve security.

4.   **Responsible Disclosure:** If sensitive data is accessed during post-exploitation activities, ethical hackers have a

responsibility to report and handle the data ethically and follow responsible disclosure procedures.

Conclusion

Post-exploitation techniques are the bridge between penetration and control in ethical hacking. Ethical hackers employ these techniques not as ends in themselves, but as means to deepen their understanding, uncover vulnerabilities, and ultimately fortify the security of digital systems and networks. Responsible and ethical conduct, adherence to legal and ethical guidelines, and expert utilization of post-exploitation techniques and tools are essential in the successful execution of this critical phase of ethical hacking, ensuring the protection of digital realms against evolving cyber threats while respecting ethical boundaries.

E. Privilege Escalation: Ascending the Hierarchy of Access

In the intricate realm of ethical hacking, where security assessments require a deep dive into system vulnerabilities, privilege escalation emerges as a crucial technique. It represents the process of elevating one's access rights or permissions within a compromised system or network. Ethical hackers employ privilege escalation to gain higher-level privileges, unlock additional functionality, and further assess security postures.

The Significance of Privilege Escalation

Privilege escalation holds significant relevance in ethical hacking for several compelling reasons:

1. **Enhanced Control:** By elevating privileges, ethical hackers gain more extensive control over the compromised system. This allows them to perform tasks that were previously restricted, such as modifying critical system files.

2. **Access to Sensitive Data:** Higher-level privileges often grant access to sensitive data, confidential files, or protected resources, which can be valuable for security assessments and risk evaluations.

3. **Expanded Attack Surface:** Privilege escalation can open doors to new vulnerabilities and attack vectors, as higher-privileged accounts or processes may interact with critical system components.

4. **Proof of Concept:** Demonstrating privilege escalation serves as a "proof of concept" (PoC) to illustrate to stakeholders the potential risks of unauthorized privilege escalation and the importance of mitigating such vulnerabilities.

Methods of Privilege Escalation

Ethical hackers employ various methods and techniques for privilege escalation, depending on the specific target, operating system, and security configurations. Common methods include:

1.   **Exploiting Known Vulnerabilities:** Ethical hackers may leverage known vulnerabilities or misconfigurations within the system or application to gain elevated privileges. This could involve exploiting unpatched software or weak access controls.

2.   **Executing Arbitrary Code:** In some cases, ethical hackers execute malicious code or scripts within the context of a lower-privileged account or application. If the system lacks proper security mechanisms, this code may run with higher privileges, leading to privilege escalation.

3.   **Abusing Weak Permissions:** Ethical hackers may discover files, directories, or services with weak permissions that allow them to access restricted resources or execute privileged actions.

4.   **Password Cracking:** In situations where credentials are involved, ethical hackers might attempt to crack passwords or obtain credentials through other means (e.g., social engineering) to gain access to higher-privileged accounts.

5.   **Kernel Exploitation:** On some systems, kernel-level vulnerabilities can be exploited to escalate privileges to the highest level, typically "root" or "administrator."

6.   **Bypassing UAC (User Account Control):** On Windows systems, ethical hackers can attempt to bypass the User Account Control (UAC) mechanism, which enforces security restrictions on non-administrator accounts.

Tools and Techniques for Privilege Escalation

Ethical hackers have access to various tools, techniques, and scripts to aid in privilege escalation:

1.   **Enumeration Tools:** Enumeration tools like LinEnum and WinEnum assist in gathering information about the system and identifying potential privilege escalation vectors.

2.   **Exploit Frameworks:** Frameworks like Metasploit contain modules for privilege escalation, making it easier to automate and streamline the process.

3.   **Local Exploits:** Local privilege escalation exploits target vulnerabilities within the local system to gain higher privileges.

4.   **Kernel Exploits:** Kernel exploits specifically target vulnerabilities in the operating system's kernel to escalate privileges to the highest level.

5.   **Scheduled Tasks and Cron Jobs:** Ethical hackers may examine scheduled tasks and cron jobs for misconfigurations that could allow them to execute code with higher privileges.

Ethical Considerations in Privilege Escalation

Privilege escalation in ethical hacking must adhere to strict ethical and legal guidelines:

1.   **Authorization:** Ethical hackers must have explicit authorization from the organization or system owner to engage in privilege escalation activities. Unauthorized actions are illegal and unethical.

2.   **Minimize Harm:** Ethical hackers should aim to minimize disruption, damage, or data exposure while conducting privilege escalation activities. The goal is to demonstrate the existence of risks without causing undue harm.

3.   **Documentation:** All privilege escalation activities, including findings, actions taken, and recommendations, must be thoroughly documented to provide transparency, accountability, and the foundation for remediation.

4.   **Responsible Disclosure:** Ethical hackers have a responsibility to report and handle identified privilege escalation vulnerabilities responsibly, following ethical disclosure procedures.

Conclusion

Privilege escalation is the process of ascending the hierarchy of access within a compromised system or network. Ethical hackers employ this technique not as an end but as a means to uncover, assess, and improve the security of digital systems and networks. Responsible and ethical conduct, adherence to legal and ethical guidelines, and expert utilization of privilege escalation techniques and tools are essential in the successful execution of this critical phase of ethical hacking. The ultimate aim is to fortify digital realms against evolving cyber threats while respecting ethical boundaries and maintaining the highest standards of security and ethics.

Chapter 7:

Web Application Testing

In today's interconnected digital landscape, web applications have become the backbone of countless services and businesses. However, this widespread reliance on web applications also presents a significant security challenge. Web application testing is the sentinel at the gate, the shield against the myriad of threats lurking in the virtual world.

Guardians of Digital Gateways

Web applications are the lifeblood of online commerce, communication, and collaboration. From e-commerce platforms to social media networks, web applications enable us to connect, transact, and share seamlessly. Yet, beneath their user-friendly interfaces lies a complex world of vulnerabilities and potential exploits.

Web application testing is the art of systematically probing, analyzing, and fortifying these digital gateways. It is the guardian of sensitive user data, the protector of financial transactions, and the defender against malicious hackers seeking to exploit weaknesses in the code.

The Complexity of Web Applications

Web applications are dynamic, intricate, and constantly evolving. Their complexity, combined with the rapid pace of development, creates an ever-shifting security landscape. Web application testing must adapt and evolve in tandem, keeping pace with the latest attack vectors and vulnerabilities.

This chapter embarks on a journey through the realm of web application testing. We will explore the methodologies, tools, and best practices that ethical hackers and security professionals employ to assess the security of web applications comprehensively. From identifying common vulnerabilities to understanding secure coding practices, this chapter equips you with the knowledge and skills to safeguard the digital gateways of the modern world.

Join us as we unravel the complexities of web application testing, revealing the techniques and strategies used to ensure that these digital gateways remain resilient against cyber threats. Together, we will explore the critical role of ethical hacking in securing the digital future, one web application at a time.

A. Web Application Architecture: Building the Foundations of the Digital World

Web applications are the lifeblood of the digital age, serving as the interface between users and the vast universe of online services. Behind every web application's user-friendly interface lies a complex and meticulously designed architecture. Web application architecture defines how the various components of an application interact and work together to deliver functionality, data, and a seamless user experience.

Understanding the Significance of Web Application Architecture

Web application architecture is the blueprint that underpins the development, functionality, and security of modern web applications. Its significance stems from several key factors:

1.   **User Experience:** A well-designed architecture ensures a smooth and responsive user experience. It determines how efficiently data is processed, presented, and interacted with.

2.   **Scalability:** Scalability is essential to accommodate growing user bases and increasing traffic. The architecture must be designed to handle increased load and demand without sacrificing performance.

3.   **Security:** Security is paramount in the digital age, and the architecture plays a crucial role in safeguarding sensitive data, protecting against vulnerabilities, and implementing access controls.

4.   **Maintainability:** The architecture influences the ease with which developers can maintain, update, and add new features to an application. A well-structured architecture simplifies these tasks.

Components of Web Application Architecture

Web application architecture comprises several key components that work together harmoniously:

1.   **Client:** The client is the user interface through which users interact with the application. It can be a web browser, a mobile app, or any other client-side technology.

2.   **Server:** The server is responsible for processing requests from clients, managing the application's logic, and interacting with the database. It can be a physical server or a cloud-based server.

3.   **Database:** The database stores and manages the application's data. It can be a relational database (e.g., MySQL, PostgreSQL), a NoSQL database (e.g., MongoDB, Cassandra), or a combination of both.

4.   **Application Logic:** The application logic defines the behavior and functionality of the web application. It includes business rules, workflows, and processing logic.

5.   **Web Server:** The web server handles HTTP requests

and responses. It can be a separate component or integrated into the server.

6.   **APIs (Application Programming Interfaces):** APIs allow different components of the application to communicate and share data. They are essential for integrating third-party services, mobile apps, and other systems.

Types of Web Application Architectures

Web applications can be built using various architectural patterns, each with its strengths and use cases:

1.   **Single-Tier (Monolithic) Architecture:** In this traditional architecture, all components of the application are tightly coupled and run on a single server. It's simple but may lack scalability and maintainability.

2.   **Two-Tier (Client-Server) Architecture:** This architecture separates the client and server components, allowing for better scalability and flexibility.

3.   **Three-Tier Architecture:** The three-tier architecture further separates the application into three layers: presentation (client), application logic (server), and data storage (database). It offers improved modularity and scalability.

4.   **Microservices Architecture:** In this modern approach, the application is divided into small, independent

services that communicate via APIs. It enhances scalability, maintainability, and flexibility.

5.   **Serverless Architecture:** In a serverless architecture, the cloud provider manages infrastructure, and developers focus solely on writing code. It's highly scalable and cost-efficient.

Challenges in Web Application Architecture

Building robust web application architectures comes with its set of challenges:

1.   **Scalability:** Ensuring the application can handle traffic spikes and growth in the user base.

2.   **Security:** Protecting against threats like SQL injection, cross-site scripting (XSS), and data breaches.

3.   **Performance:** Optimizing application performance, minimizing latency, and ensuring fast response times.

4.   **Maintainability:** Making it easy for developers to update and expand the application without introducing bugs or disruptions.

5.   **Data Management:** Effectively managing and securing sensitive user data.

Conclusion

Web application architecture serves as the foundation for the digital world, influencing everything from user experiences to security and scalability. Understanding the complexities of web application architecture is essential for developers, architects, and security professionals to design, build, and maintain applications that meet the demands of the modern digital landscape. A well-structured and thoughtfully designed architecture is the key to success in the ever-evolving world of web applications.

B. Common Web Application Vulnerabilities: Unmasking the Achilles' Heels

Web applications are the backbone of the digital world, empowering users to interact, transact, and communicate seamlessly. Yet, beneath the surface of these powerful tools lie vulnerabilities that, if left unaddressed, can expose sensitive data, compromise security, and lead to significant consequences. Understanding these common web application vulnerabilities is crucial for developers, security professionals, and ethical hackers seeking to protect digital assets and user privacy.

1. SQL Injection (SQLi): The Data Thief's Gateway

SQL Injection is a prevalent and potentially devastating vulnerability. It occurs when attackers insert malicious SQL queries into user inputs, tricking the application into executing unintended database actions. This vulnerability can lead to unauthorized access, data theft, and even full control of the database.

2. Cross-Site Scripting (XSS): The Scripted Saboteur

Cross-Site Scripting is a vulnerability that allows attackers to inject malicious scripts into web pages viewed by other users. These scripts can steal sensitive data (such as cookies) or perform actions on behalf of the victim, potentially leading to account hijacking, data theft, or defacement of websites.

3. Cross-Site Request Forgery (CSRF): The Deceptive Requester

Cross-Site Request Forgery is an attack that tricks users into executing unwanted actions on a different website without their consent. Attackers can force users to perform actions like changing their email address or making unauthorized transactions, potentially leading to financial loss or unauthorized data changes.

4. Insecure Deserialization: The Shape-Shifting Vulnerability

Insecure Deserialization is a vulnerability that arises when an application accepts serialized data from untrusted sources without proper validation. Attackers can manipulate serialized objects to execute malicious code, potentially leading to remote code execution, data tampering, or even denial of service.

5. Security Misconfigurations: The Open Door Policy

Security misconfigurations occur when applications or systems are not properly configured, leaving them vulnerable to exploitation. Common issues include default credentials, unnecessary services running, overly permissive permissions, and exposed sensitive information like error messages.

6. Broken Authentication: The Identity Crisis

Broken Authentication vulnerabilities arise when an application fails to adequately protect user credentials, sessions, or tokens. Attackers can exploit these flaws to impersonate users, gain unauthorized access to accounts, and compromise sensitive data.

7. Insecure Direct Object References (IDOR): The Unauthorized Access Route

Insecure Direct Object References occur when an application exposes internal implementation objects, such as files or database records, to users without proper authorization. Attackers can manipulate references to access unauthorized data, potentially leading to data leaks or unauthorized actions.

8. XML External Entity (XXE) Injection: The XML Whisperer

XXE Injection exploits the processing of XML documents by an application, allowing attackers to include malicious entities or external references. This can lead to data disclosure, denial of service, or remote code execution.

9. Unvalidated Redirects and Forwards: The Misguided Path

Unvalidated redirects and forwards vulnerabilities occur when applications allow users to specify a URL to which they will be redirected. Attackers can manipulate these URLs to trick users into visiting malicious sites, potentially leading to phishing attacks or malware downloads.

10. Broken Access Control: The Unauthorized Explorer

Broken Access Control issues occur when an application fails to enforce proper access controls, allowing unauthorized users to access restricted resources or perform actions. This can lead to data exposure, privilege escalation, and unauthorized operations.

Conclusion

Common web application vulnerabilities pose significant risks to the security and integrity of digital systems and user data. Understanding these vulnerabilities is the first step in addressing and mitigating them effectively. Developers, security professionals, and ethical hackers must be vigilant in identifying and remediating these weaknesses to ensure that web applications remain resilient against evolving cyber threats, protecting both digital assets and user trust in the ever-connected digital world.

C. Web Application Scanning Tools: The Sentry of Cybersecurity

In the digital age, web applications are the heart of online services and businesses. However, their prevalence also makes them prime targets for cyberattacks. To fortify the digital gates and uncover vulnerabilities, security professionals and ethical hackers rely on web application scanning tools. These tools act as vigilant sentinels, systematically probing applications for weaknesses, ensuring robust security, and safeguarding sensitive data.

The Significance of Web Application Scanning Tools

Web application scanning tools are indispensable for several compelling reasons:

1.   **Comprehensive Assessment:** These tools automate the process of identifying vulnerabilities, ensuring that no stone is left unturned. They perform in-depth scans, including both automated and manual testing, to detect a wide range of security

issues.

2.   **Efficiency:** Manual testing can be time-consuming and error-prone. Web application scanning tools enhance efficiency by quickly and accurately identifying vulnerabilities, allowing security teams to focus on remediation.

3.   **Consistency:** These tools maintain consistency in testing processes, ensuring that tests are executed uniformly across different parts of an application, which can be challenging with manual testing.

4.   **Reporting:** Web application scanning tools provide detailed reports, including identified vulnerabilities, their severity, and recommended remediation steps. These reports aid in prioritizing and addressing issues.

5.   **Continuous Monitoring:** Many tools offer continuous monitoring capabilities, allowing organizations to regularly assess the security of their web applications and address new vulnerabilities as they arise.

Types of Web Application Scanning Tools

Web application scanning tools come in various types, each serving specific purposes:

1.   **Static Application Security Testing (SAST):** SAST tools analyze source code, bytecode, or binary code to identify

vulnerabilities, design flaws, and coding errors. They offer insights during the development phase.

2.   **Dynamic Application Security Testing (DAST):** DAST tools assess running applications from the outside, mimicking real-world attacks. They identify vulnerabilities in the runtime environment, such as SQL injection or XSS.

3.   **Interactive Application Security Testing (IAST):** IAST tools combine elements of both SAST and DAST. They monitor applications in real time during testing and provide feedback to developers while identifying runtime vulnerabilities.

4.   **Web Application Firewall (WAF):** A WAF is a security appliance or software that filters and monitors HTTP requests to a web application. While not a scanning tool per se, it acts as a protective layer against known attack patterns.

5.   **API Security Testing Tools:** As APIs play an increasingly critical role in web applications, specialized tools assess API security, looking for vulnerabilities like broken authentication or insecure endpoints.

Features of Web Application Scanning Tools

Web application scanning tools offer a range of features and capabilities:

1.   **Scanning:** Tools scan web applications for a wide

array of vulnerabilities, including SQL injection, Cross-Site Scripting (XSS), Cross-Site Request Forgery (CSRF), and more.

2.   **Authentication:** Many tools support authentication mechanisms to assess the application from the perspective of different user roles, such as admin, authenticated user, or guest.

3.   **Reporting:** Detailed reports are generated, outlining identified vulnerabilities, their severity, and recommendations for remediation.

4.   **Customization:** Users can often customize scanning parameters and testing policies to suit their application's unique requirements.

5.   **Integration:** Many tools integrate with development and DevOps environments, allowing for automated testing during the software development lifecycle.

Challenges and Considerations

While web application scanning tools are invaluable, they come with challenges and considerations:

1.   **False Positives and Negatives:** Tools may generate false positives (identifying vulnerabilities that don't exist) or miss certain vulnerabilities (false negatives). Human analysis is often necessary to validate findings.

2.　　**Complexity:** Some tools can be complex to set up and configure, requiring expertise to use effectively.

3.　　**Continuous Monitoring:** Regular scans are essential to identify new vulnerabilities. Continuous monitoring capabilities should be considered when selecting a tool.

4.　　**False Confidence:** Overreliance on scanning tools without validating findings can lead to a false sense of security. Human expertise is crucial to understanding and addressing vulnerabilities.

Conclusion

Web application scanning tools are indispensable assets in the defense against cyber threats. They empower organizations to systematically identify and address vulnerabilities, ensuring the security and integrity of web applications. However, these tools are most effective when used in conjunction with human expertise and a robust cybersecurity strategy. With the right tools and practices in place, organizations can confidently navigate the digital landscape, safeguarding their digital assets and user trust.

D. Secure Coding Practices: Building Fortresses in the Digital World

In the ever-connected digital landscape, where web applications and software systems form the backbone of modern interactions, security is paramount. Secure coding practices serve as the foundation upon which robust, resilient, and trustworthy software is built. These practices are the artisans' tools for crafting digital fortresses that protect against an array of threats, from hackers seeking to exploit vulnerabilities to data breaches that can compromise sensitive information.

The Significance of Secure Coding Practices

Secure coding practices are of paramount significance for several compelling reasons:

1.   **Prevention of Vulnerabilities:** These practices proactively address vulnerabilities at the source code level, minimizing the likelihood of security breaches and mitigating the associated risks.

2.   **Cost-Efficiency:** Early identification and resolution of security issues are more cost-effective than addressing vulnerabilities after deployment. Secure coding practices reduce the potential financial burden of post-release security patching.

3.   **User Trust:** Secure software instills user confidence, fostering trust and loyalty. Users are more likely to engage with and return to applications they perceive as secure.

4.   **Legal and Compliance Requirements:** Many industries and regions have legal and regulatory requirements for

data protection and privacy. Secure coding practices help ensure compliance with these mandates.

5. **Reputation Management:** Security incidents can tarnish an organization's reputation. Adhering to secure coding practices safeguards an organization's image and credibility.

Key Secure Coding Practices

Secure coding practices encompass a wide array of techniques and principles. Here are some key practices:

1. **Input Validation:** Always validate input from users and external sources to prevent injection attacks like SQL injection and Cross-Site Scripting (XSS).

2. **Authentication and Authorization:** Implement strong authentication mechanisms and ensure that users can only access resources for which they are authorized.

3. **Session Management:** Use secure session management techniques to protect against session fixation and session hijacking attacks.

4. **Data Encryption:** Encrypt sensitive data at rest and in transit using strong encryption algorithms.

5. **Error Handling:** Avoid revealing sensitive information in error messages and logs. Provide meaningful, non-

disclosure error messages to users.

6.   **Secure Configuration:** Ensure that your application and underlying components are configured securely. Remove or disable unnecessary services and features.

7.   **Access Control:** Implement the principle of least privilege, granting users the minimum level of access required for their tasks.

8.   **Code Reviews:** Conduct code reviews to identify security flaws, vulnerabilities, and coding mistakes. Involve experienced developers or security experts in the process.

9.   **Secure Development Frameworks:** Leverage secure development frameworks and libraries that have built-in security controls and best practices.

10.   **Regular Updates and Patching:** Keep all software components up-to-date with security patches and updates to mitigate known vulnerabilities.

11.   **Cross-Origin Resource Sharing (CORS):** Implement proper CORS policies to control which domains can access your web application's resources.

12.   **API Security:** Secure APIs by using authentication, authorization, rate limiting, and input validation.

Challenges and Considerations

Despite the clear benefits of secure coding practices, they come with challenges and considerations:

1.   **Awareness and Training:** Developers must be aware of security best practices and receive training to apply them effectively.

2.   **Time Constraints:** Developing secure code may require additional time and effort, which can be a challenge in fast-paced development environments.

3.   **Changing Threat Landscape:** The threat landscape evolves continuously, requiring regular updates to secure coding practices to address new threats.

4.   **Legacy Code:** Retrofitting security into legacy codebases can be challenging. It may require substantial effort to identify and remediate vulnerabilities.

Conclusion

Secure coding practices are the linchpin of cybersecurity in the digital age. They provide the means to proactively protect against a wide range of threats and vulnerabilities that could compromise sensitive data and trust. While implementing secure coding practices may require investment in training and additional development time, the long-term benefits far outweigh the costs.

Organizations that prioritize secure coding practices not only fortify their digital fortresses but also build a reputation for reliability, trustworthiness, and resilience in the face of evolving cyber threats.

Chapter 8:

Wireless Network Hacking

In an increasingly wireless world, where convenience meets connectivity, wireless networks have become the lifeblood of modern communication. Yet, beneath the convenience lies a realm of vulnerabilities and potential exploits. "Wireless Network Hacking" is the art of unraveling the invisible threads of radio waves that connect our devices, seeking vulnerabilities, and understanding how attackers can breach the digital walls that safeguard our wireless ecosystems.

The Wireless Landscape: A Tapestry of Opportunities and Risks

Wireless networks have redefined how we connect, work, and play. From the Wi-Fi that powers our homes to the cellular networks that enable global communication, the wireless landscape is a tapestry of opportunities and risks. It offers the freedom to roam untethered but also presents vulnerabilities that savvy hackers can exploit.

This chapter embarks on a journey through the intriguing world of wireless network hacking. We will delve into the methodologies, tools, and techniques employed by both ethical hackers and malicious actors to navigate the wireless spectrum. From cracking Wi-Fi passwords to understanding encryption protocols, this chapter equips you with the knowledge and skills to assess and secure wireless networks in an increasingly wireless-dependent world.

Join us as we uncover the intricacies of wireless network hacking, revealing the techniques and strategies used to ensure that the digital tapestry of wireless communication remains both robust and secure. Together, we will explore the vital role of ethical hacking in safeguarding our wireless future, one connection at a time.

A. Wireless Security Protocols: Fortifying the Airwaves

Wireless networks have revolutionized the way we connect, enabling unprecedented mobility and convenience. However, the openness of the airwaves also exposes wireless communications to potential eavesdropping, unauthorized access, and other security threats. Wireless security protocols serve as the digital sentinels, safeguarding the integrity, confidentiality, and availability of data transmitted through the invisible realm of radio waves.

The Need for Wireless Security Protocols

Wireless security protocols are of paramount importance for several compelling reasons:

1.   **Data Confidentiality:** Without robust security measures, wireless communications can be intercepted by malicious actors, leading to the exposure of sensitive data.

2.   **Privacy Protection:** Users expect their wireless communications to remain private. Security protocols help ensure that their conversations and data remain confidential.

3.   **Authentication:** Wireless security protocols provide mechanisms for verifying the identity of both users and devices, preventing unauthorized access.

4.   **Data Integrity:** Security protocols detect and prevent data tampering during transmission, ensuring that data remains unaltered and trustworthy.

5.   **Availability:** Protecting wireless networks against attacks helps maintain network availability, preventing disruptions and downtime.

Common Wireless Security Protocols

Several wireless security protocols have been developed over the years to address various security concerns. Here are some of the most common ones:

1.   **Wired Equivalent Privacy (WEP):** WEP was one of the earliest wireless security protocols. However, it is now considered highly insecure due to vulnerabilities that make it susceptible to attacks.

2.   **Wi-Fi Protected Access (WPA):** WPA improved upon WEP's shortcomings by introducing stronger encryption and security mechanisms. However, it also had vulnerabilities that led to the development of more secure variants.

3.   **WPA2:** WPA2 is currently one of the most widely used wireless security protocols. It employs strong encryption (AES) and has robust security features. However, it is not immune to advanced attacks.

4.   **WPA3:** WPA3 is the latest iteration of Wi-Fi security. It provides enhanced security through features like Simultaneous Authentication of Equals (SAE), stronger encryption, and protection against brute-force attacks.

5.   **Extensible Authentication Protocol (EAP):** EAP is a framework that allows for various authentication methods within wireless networks. It is often used with other protocols like EAP-TLS or EAP-PEAP to strengthen authentication.

6.   **802.1X:** This is an IEEE standard for network access

control that is often used in conjunction with EAP for secure authentication in Wi-Fi networks.

7.   **Virtual Private Networks (VPNs):** While not a wireless-specific protocol, VPNs are commonly used to secure wireless connections by encrypting data traffic between the client and the server.

Challenges and Considerations

Wireless security protocols, despite their critical role, come with challenges and considerations:

1.   **Backward Compatibility:** Older devices may not support the latest security protocols, potentially creating security gaps in the network.

2.   **Key Management:** Proper key management is crucial for the effectiveness of wireless security protocols. Weak or mishandled keys can compromise security.

3.   **Emerging Threats:** The threat landscape evolves continuously. Security protocols must adapt to address new vulnerabilities and attack techniques.

4.   **User Education:** Users should be educated about the importance of strong wireless security practices, including password management and device security.

5.   **Configuration Errors:** Misconfigurations can weaken the effectiveness of security protocols. Organizations must ensure proper configuration of security settings.

Conclusion

Wireless security protocols play a pivotal role in ensuring the confidentiality, integrity, and availability of wireless communications. They are the digital guardians that protect data as it traverses the airwaves. While the landscape of wireless security is ever-evolving, staying informed about the latest developments in security protocols and implementing best practices is essential for maintaining the security and privacy of wireless networks in our increasingly connected world.

B. WEP, WPA, WPA2 Cracking: Unveiling the Weaknesses in Wireless Security

Wireless networks have become an integral part of modern connectivity, offering the convenience of untethered access to the digital world. However, the security of these networks has been a constant concern due to vulnerabilities in earlier encryption standards like Wired Equivalent Privacy (WEP) and the subsequent Wi-Fi Protected Access (WPA) protocols, including WPA and WPA2. Cracking these encryption methods has been a focus for both malicious actors and ethical hackers, revealing the importance of robust wireless security measures.

WEP (Wired Equivalent Privacy) Cracking: A Flawed Foundation

WEP was one of the first encryption protocols used to secure Wi-Fi networks. However, it was deeply flawed from the outset due to several key weaknesses:

1.   **Static Encryption Keys:** WEP used static encryption keys, which meant that the same key was used for all data packets. This predictability made it vulnerable to key recovery attacks.

2.   **Weak Encryption:** WEP relied on the RC4 encryption algorithm with a 40- or 104-bit key size. Advances in computing power made it feasible for attackers to crack these keys through brute-force or statistical attacks.

3.   **Initialization Vector (IV) Vulnerabilities:** WEP used a 24-bit IV, which was too short, allowing attackers to carry out statistical attacks and eventually recover the encryption key.

Cracking WEP typically involves capturing a sufficient number of data packets and then running attacks to discover the encryption key. Tools like Aircrack-ng and Kismet are commonly used for WEP cracking. Due to its severe vulnerabilities, WEP should never be used to secure wireless networks.

WPA (Wi-Fi Protected Access) Cracking: A Step Forward, but Not Immune

In response to WEP's weaknesses, WPA was introduced, offering improved security through Temporal Key Integrity Protocol (TKIP) and Message Integrity Check (MIC). However, WPA also had vulnerabilities:

1.   **TKIP Vulnerabilities:** TKIP, while more secure than WEP, had its own vulnerabilities. Attackers could exploit these to launch attacks like the Beck-Tews attack, which could lead to key recovery.

2.   **Weak Passwords:** Many WPA-protected networks used weak or easily guessable passwords, making them susceptible to dictionary attacks or brute-force attacks.

3.   **Offline Attacks:** Attackers could capture WPA handshake packets and then use offline attacks to crack the network's passphrase.

Tools like Aircrack-ng, Reaver, and coWPAtty were commonly used for WPA cracking. While WPA was a significant improvement over WEP, it was not immune to attacks.

WPA2 (Wi-Fi Protected Access II) Cracking: A Struggle for Perfection

WPA2 addressed many of the vulnerabilities of WEP and WPA

by using the Advanced Encryption Standard (AES) and Counter Mode Cipher Block Chaining Message Authentication Code Protocol (CCMP). However, WPA2 also had its share of vulnerabilities:

1. **Brute-Force Attacks:** Weak passwords and poorly chosen passphrases could still be susceptible to brute-force attacks.

2. **WPS Vulnerabilities:** Wi-Fi Protected Setup (WPS), a feature designed for user-friendly network setup, had serious security issues that could allow attackers to easily crack WPA2 networks if WPS was enabled.

Cracking WPA2 often involves capturing a handshake when a device connects to the network and then using tools like Hashcat, aircrack-ng, or Reaver to attempt to recover the passphrase.

Mitigating Cracking Attacks

To defend against cracking attacks, several measures can be taken:

1. **Use WPA3:** WPA3 is the latest Wi-Fi security protocol and offers improved security features, making it harder for attackers to crack wireless networks.

2. **Use Strong Passwords:** Employ long, complex, and unique passphrases or use a passphrase manager to generate strong

keys.

3.   **Disable WPS:** If your router supports it, disable WPS to prevent attacks leveraging WPS vulnerabilities.

4.   **Regularly Update Firmware:** Keep your router's firmware up to date to patch any security vulnerabilities.

5.   **Monitor Network Activity:** Use network monitoring tools to detect suspicious activity and unauthorized access attempts.

In conclusion, while WEP, WPA, and WPA2 have all been targets for cracking attacks, WPA3 represents a significant step forward in wireless security. However, it's crucial to remain vigilant, keep systems updated, and use strong security practices to defend against potential threats in an ever-evolving security landscape.

C. Rogue Access Points: The Unseen Threats to Wireless Networks

Wireless networks have redefined how we connect and communicate, offering unparalleled convenience and mobility. However, they also introduce unique security challenges, one of which is the presence of rogue access points. Rogue access points are unauthorized or maliciously deployed wireless access points that can undermine the security of networks, compromise data integrity, and pose significant risks to organizations and individuals.

Understanding Rogue Access Points

A rogue access point is a wireless access point that is deployed on a network without the explicit authorization or knowledge of the network administrator. Rogue access points can take various forms:

1.   **Maliciously Deployed APs:** These are intentionally set up by malicious actors with the intent to eavesdrop on network traffic, steal data, or launch attacks.

2.   **Unintentional APs:** In some cases, employees or users might unknowingly set up their own wireless access points, creating unintentional rogue access points. These can be equally dangerous, as they may lack proper security configurations.

3.   **Ad Hoc Networks:** In ad hoc networking, devices connect directly to each other without a central access point. If not properly secured, ad hoc networks can become rogue access points within a corporate network.

Risks and Implications

The presence of rogue access points poses several risks and implications:

1.   **Security Breaches:** Rogue access points can facilitate unauthorized access to a network, allowing attackers to intercept traffic, launch attacks, or gain unauthorized entry to sensitive systems.

2.   **Data Theft:** Attackers can exploit rogue access points to capture data transmitted over the network, potentially leading to data theft or exposure of confidential information.

3.   **Malware Distribution:** Rogue access points can be used as vectors for distributing malware or conducting man-in-the-middle attacks, infecting connected devices with malicious software.

4.   **Network Degradation:** Unintentional rogue access points can interfere with the normal operation of the wireless network, causing performance issues and disrupting legitimate connections.

5.   **Regulatory Compliance:** Organizations that fail to address rogue access points may violate industry-specific regulations and compliance requirements related to network security and data protection.

Detecting and Mitigating Rogue Access Points

Detecting and mitigating rogue access points is essential to maintain the security of wireless networks. Here are some strategies and tools for addressing this threat:

1.   **Wireless Intrusion Detection Systems (WIDS):** WIDS solutions are designed to detect rogue access points and unauthorized devices on a wireless network. They use a combination of signature-based and anomaly-based detection methods.

2.   **Regular Scanning:** Periodic scans of the wireless spectrum can identify unauthorized access points. Wireless scanning tools like Kismet, Airodump-ng, or commercial WIDS solutions can be used for this purpose.

3.   **802.1X Authentication:** Implement IEEE 802.1X authentication, which requires users and devices to authenticate before accessing the network. This helps prevent unauthorized access.

4.   **Wireless Network Policy:** Establish and enforce a wireless network usage policy that prohibits the deployment of unauthorized access points. Educate employees and users about the risks associated with rogue access points.

5.   **Network Segmentation:** Segmenting the network can limit the impact of rogue access points. Use VLANs and access control lists (ACLs) to isolate critical network segments from less secure areas.

6.   **Active Detection and Remediation:** Some WIDS solutions can actively block or disconnect rogue access points from the network, providing an immediate response to detected threats.

Conclusion

Rogue access points represent a stealthy and pervasive threat to wireless networks. Their presence can lead to security breaches, data theft, and network disruptions. To mitigate these risks, organizations must adopt proactive measures, including the use of intrusion detection systems, regular scanning, and robust network policies. By addressing rogue access points, organizations can maintain the integrity and security of their wireless networks in an era of ever-increasing connectivity.

D. Wireless Security Best Practices: Safeguarding the Airwaves

Wireless networks have become an integral part of our digital lives, offering the freedom to connect from anywhere. However, this convenience also brings a unique set of security challenges. To protect sensitive data and maintain the integrity of wireless networks, it's crucial to follow wireless security best practices. These practices form the foundation of a robust defense against potential threats.

1. Strong Authentication and Encryption

• **Use WPA3:** Whenever possible, use the latest Wi-Fi Protected Access (WPA3) protocol. WPA3 introduces stronger encryption and security features, making it significantly more resilient against attacks compared to its predecessors, WPA and WPA2.

• **Enable 802.1X Authentication:** Implement IEEE 802.1X authentication, which requires users and devices to authenticate before accessing the network. This adds an extra layer of security by verifying the identity of connected devices.

• **Use Strong Passwords and Passphrases:** Encourage users to create strong and unique passwords or passphrases for their Wi-Fi networks. Avoid default or easily guessable passwords.

2. Network Segmentation

• **VLANs and Subnetting:** Segment your wireless network using Virtual LANs (VLANs) and subnetting. This isolates critical network segments from less secure areas, reducing the potential impact of security breaches.

3. Regular Updates and Patching

• **Firmware Updates:** Keep wireless routers and access points up to date with the latest firmware and security patches.

Manufacturers often release updates to address vulnerabilities.

4. Disable Unnecessary Services

• **Disable WPS:** Wi-Fi Protected Setup (WPS) has known vulnerabilities that can be exploited by attackers. Disable it on your router unless it's absolutely necessary for compatibility.

• **Guest Network Isolation:** If you offer a guest network, ensure it is isolated from your primary network to prevent unauthorized access to sensitive resources.

5. Strong Physical Security

• **Physical Access Control:** Secure your wireless access points and routers in locked cabinets or secure locations to prevent physical tampering or unauthorized access.

6. Intrusion Detection and Prevention

• **Wireless Intrusion Detection Systems (WIDS):** Deploy a WIDS to monitor the wireless spectrum for rogue access points and unauthorized devices. WIDS can provide alerts and automatic responses to detected threats.

7. Monitor Network Activity

• **Regular Network Monitoring:** Implement network monitoring tools to detect unusual or suspicious activity on your wireless network. Anomalies can be indicative of security breaches.

8. User Education and Training

- **Security Awareness:** Educate users about the importance of wireless security. Teach them how to recognize phishing attempts, the risks of connecting to unsecured networks, and the importance of strong passwords.

- **Safe Wi-Fi Practices:** Encourage users to connect only to trusted networks and avoid public Wi-Fi networks unless they are using a Virtual Private Network (VPN).

9. Strong Encryption for Sensitive Data

- **End-to-End Encryption:** When transmitting sensitive data over a wireless network, ensure that end-to-end encryption protocols, such as HTTPS for web traffic, are in place.

10. Plan for Incident Response

- **Incident Response Plan:** Develop an incident response plan specifically for wireless network security incidents. Be prepared to isolate affected devices, change passwords, and investigate breaches.

11. Regular Security Audits and Testing

- **Penetration Testing:** Conduct regular penetration testing and security audits to identify vulnerabilities and weaknesses in your wireless network. Address any issues promptly.

12. Remote Management Security

- **Secure Remote Access:** If you allow remote management of network devices, secure it with strong authentication and encryption. Disable remote access features when not needed.

13. Disable Unnecessary Features

- **Unused Features:** Disable any unused features or services on your wireless router or access points. Reducing the attack surface can enhance security.

14. Log and Analyze Data

- **Logging:** Enable logging on your network devices and analyze logs for signs of suspicious activity. Logs can provide valuable information during incident investigations.

15. Guest Network Security

- **Isolate Guest Networks:** If you offer a guest network, isolate it from your primary network to prevent unauthorized access to sensitive resources.

Conclusion

Wireless security best practices are crucial for safeguarding the airwaves and ensuring the integrity and confidentiality of wireless communications. By implementing these measures, organizations and individuals can mitigate the risks associated with wireless networks and maintain a secure and reliable wireless environment in an increasingly connected world.

Chapter 9:

Mobile and IoT Hacking

In an era where our lives are intricately intertwined with mobile devices and the Internet of Things (IoT), the realm of cybersecurity extends far beyond traditional computers. Mobile phones and IoT devices have become ubiquitous companions, offering convenience, automation, and interconnectivity. However, with this ubiquity comes an expanded attack surface, inviting the attention of both ethical hackers seeking to bolster security and malicious actors seeking to exploit vulnerabilities.

The Convergence of Mobile and IoT

Mobile devices and IoT technologies have ushered in an era of unprecedented connectivity. Smartphones have evolved into powerful pocket-sized computers, while IoT devices have permeated our homes, workplaces, and daily lives. From smart thermostats and wearables to connected vehicles and industrial sensors, the IoT ecosystem spans a multitude of industries.

This chapter embarks on a journey into the intriguing world of mobile and IoT hacking. We will delve into the methodologies, vulnerabilities, and countermeasures that characterize the landscape of hacking these interconnected devices. From mobile application vulnerabilities to the unique challenges of securing IoT ecosystems, this chapter equips you with the knowledge and skills to assess and enhance the security of mobile and IoT devices.

Join us as we navigate the intricate web of mobile and IoT hacking, uncovering the techniques and strategies used by both ethical hackers and adversaries. Together, we will explore the vital role of ethical hacking in safeguarding our digital lives and shaping the future of mobile and IoT security.

A. Mobile Security Threats: Navigating the Perils of the Mobile Frontier

Mobile devices have revolutionized the way we live, work, and communicate. These pocket-sized powerhouses, in the form of smartphones and tablets, have become an indispensable part of modern life. However, the rapid proliferation of mobile technology has also attracted the attention of cybercriminals and threat actors, leading to a plethora of mobile security threats that can compromise our privacy, data, and digital identities.

Understanding Mobile Security Threats

Mobile security threats encompass a wide array of risks and vulnerabilities that target mobile devices and the data they contain. These threats can be broadly categorized into several key areas:

1.   **Malware and Mobile Viruses:** Malicious software (malware) designed for mobile platforms can infect devices, steal sensitive data, or perform unauthorized actions. Common types of mobile malware include Trojans, ransomware, spyware, and adware.

2.   **App-based Threats:** Mobile apps can pose security risks, especially if they are downloaded from untrusted sources or have malicious code embedded. Threats include fake or malicious apps, app vulnerabilities, and app-based phishing.

3.   **Phishing Attacks:** Phishing attacks targeting mobile users can trick them into revealing personal information, login credentials, or financial details through fraudulent emails, SMS messages, or fake websites.

4.   **Network-based Threats:** Mobile devices connect to various networks, including public Wi-Fi and cellular networks. Attackers can exploit weaknesses in these networks to intercept communications or launch attacks like man-in-the-middle (MitM) attacks.

5.   **Device Theft and Loss:** The physical loss or theft of a mobile device can lead to data breaches and unauthorized access. If not properly secured, the device's data can be compromised.

6.   **Operating System Vulnerabilities:** Vulnerabilities in mobile operating systems can be exploited by attackers to gain

unauthorized access, manipulate devices, or install malware. Prompt OS updates and patches are critical for mitigating this threat.

7.   **Jailbreaking and Rooting:** Users who attempt to remove device restrictions by jailbreaking (iOS) or rooting (Android) their devices may inadvertently expose them to security risks, as these actions bypass built-in security mechanisms.

8.   **Insecure Wi-Fi and Bluetooth:** Unsecured Wi-Fi and Bluetooth connections can expose devices to various threats, including eavesdropping and data interception.

Implications and Risks

Mobile security threats carry several significant implications and risks:

1.   **Data Breaches:** Mobile devices often contain sensitive personal and corporate data. Breaches can lead to data theft, identity theft, and financial loss.

2.   **Privacy Violations:** Unauthorized access to personal data, such as contacts, messages, and location information, can infringe upon user privacy.

3.   **Financial Loss:** Mobile threats can lead to financial fraud, unauthorized transactions, or ransom demands.

4.   **Reputation Damage:** A compromised mobile device can tarnish an individual's or organization's reputation, especially if sensitive information is exposed.

5.   **Regulatory Compliance:** Failure to secure mobile devices can result in non-compliance with data protection regulations, leading to legal and financial consequences.

Mitigation and Prevention

Mitigating mobile security threats requires a proactive approach and the implementation of security best practices:

1.   **Regular Updates:** Keep mobile operating systems and apps up to date with the latest security patches and updates.

2.   **App Security:** Download apps only from official app stores, review app permissions, and be cautious about granting excessive access.

3.   **Mobile Security Software:** Install reputable mobile security applications that offer malware scanning, anti-phishing, and anti-theft features.

4.   **Strong Authentication:** Enable strong authentication methods, such as biometrics or two-factor authentication (2FA), to protect device access.

5.   **Secure Connections:** Avoid public Wi-Fi networks

for sensitive transactions and use VPNs for secure browsing on untrusted networks.

6.   **Backup Data:** Regularly back up mobile device data to ensure data recovery in case of loss or compromise.

7.   **Educate Users:** Educate users about mobile security threats, safe browsing practices, and the importance of being cautious with emails and downloads.

8.   **Remote Wipe and Lock:** Implement remote tracking, locking, and wiping capabilities in case of device loss or theft.

Conclusion

Mobile security threats are an ever-present challenge in our increasingly mobile-dependent world. Staying informed about emerging threats, adopting best practices, and maintaining vigilance are essential steps in safeguarding mobile devices and preserving the security and privacy of personal and corporate data. As mobile technology continues to evolve, so too must our efforts to protect against evolving threats.

B. Hacking Mobile Applications: Uncovering Vulnerabilities in the Palm of Your Hand

Mobile applications have transformed the way we interact with technology, offering a myriad of functionalities from communication and productivity to entertainment and banking. However, this convenience comes with a double-edged sword. Mobile applications, like any software, are susceptible to security vulnerabilities and can be the target of various hacking techniques. Understanding how mobile applications can be compromised is crucial for both developers and users to protect against potential threats.

The Appeal of Mobile Applications

Mobile applications have become an integral part of our daily lives. They provide us with on-the-go access to a vast array of services, making our smartphones and tablets indispensable. However, this very ubiquity and the treasure trove of personal and sensitive data they often handle have made mobile applications an attractive target for hackers.

Common Mobile Application Security Threats

Mobile application security threats encompass a wide range of risks and vulnerabilities. Some of the most common threats include:

1.   **Data Leakage:** Mobile apps can inadvertently expose sensitive data, such as login credentials, personal information, and financial details, if proper data storage and encryption practices are not implemented.

2.   **Insecure Data Transmission:** Insufficient encryption during data transmission can lead to eavesdropping and interception of data between the app and its server, especially on unsecured networks.

3.   **Malicious Code Injection:** Attackers may attempt to inject malicious code into an app through various means, potentially leading to unauthorized access or control.

4.   **Authentication Flaws:** Weak or improperly implemented authentication mechanisms can allow unauthorized users to gain access to accounts or sensitive areas of the app.

5.   **Insecure APIs:** Mobile apps often interact with web services through APIs (Application Programming Interfaces). Insecure APIs can expose data and functionality, making them susceptible to abuse.

6.   **Client-Side Vulnerabilities:** Vulnerabilities on the client side of the application, such as insecure storage or inadequate input validation, can be exploited to compromise user data or device integrity.

7.   **Reverse Engineering:** Attackers may attempt to reverse engineer an app to discover its inner workings, potentially identifying vulnerabilities that can be exploited.

Hacking Techniques for Mobile Applications

Hacking mobile applications involves a range of techniques and tools, including:

1.   **Static Analysis:** This technique involves examining the source code or binary of an app without executing it. Developers and security professionals can use static analysis tools to identify vulnerabilities.

2.   **Dynamic Analysis:** Dynamic analysis involves executing the app in a controlled environment to observe its behavior and interactions with the device and network. This can reveal runtime vulnerabilities and security weaknesses.

3.   **Penetration Testing:** Ethical hackers use penetration testing to simulate attacks on mobile applications, identifying vulnerabilities and assessing their impact.

4.   **Code Review:** Security experts review the source code of the application for vulnerabilities such as improper data handling, insecure storage, and authentication issues.

5.   **API Testing:** Testing the APIs that the mobile app interacts with can uncover vulnerabilities in data transmission and interaction with external services.

6.   **Emulation and Simulation:** Using emulators or simulators, testers can replicate different device and network

conditions to evaluate how the app behaves under various scenarios.

Mitigation and Prevention

To protect against mobile application hacking, developers and organizations can implement various security practices:

1.   **Secure Coding:** Developers should follow secure coding practices, including input validation, encryption, and secure storage of sensitive data.

2.   **Regular Testing:** Conduct regular security testing, including static and dynamic analysis, penetration testing, and API testing.

3.   **Authentication and Authorization:** Implement robust authentication mechanisms and role-based access control to ensure that only authorized users can access sensitive functionality.

4.   **Use of Secure APIs:** Ensure that APIs used by the app are secure and validate input and output data.

5.   **Code Signing and Obfuscation:** Implement code signing to verify app authenticity and use code obfuscation techniques to make reverse engineering more difficult.

6.   **Security Updates:** Regularly update the app with

security patches and bug fixes to address vulnerabilities.

7.   **Education and Training:** Educate developers and users about mobile app security best practices and potential threats.

Conclusion

Mobile applications are a vital part of our connected world, offering immense convenience and functionality. However, their widespread use also makes them a prime target for hackers. Developers and organizations must prioritize mobile application security to protect user data and maintain trust. By employing secure coding practices, regular testing, and proactive security measures, the risks associated with mobile application hacking can be significantly reduced, ensuring that mobile apps remain a reliable and secure part of our digital landscape.

C. IoT Device Vulnerabilities: The Achilles' Heel of the Internet of Things

The Internet of Things (IoT) has heralded a new era of interconnected devices, from smart thermostats and wearable fitness trackers to industrial sensors and autonomous vehicles. While the promise of IoT lies in enhanced convenience, automation, and efficiency, the proliferation of these devices has also ushered in a wave of IoT device vulnerabilities. These vulnerabilities, if left unaddressed, can pose significant risks to privacy, security, and the integrity of IoT ecosystems.

The Expanding Universe of IoT

IoT devices encompass a broad spectrum of technologies, each designed to serve specific purposes and functions. From consumer-oriented IoT devices that enhance our daily lives to critical infrastructure components that power industries, the IoT ecosystem continues to expand. However, the diversity and complexity of IoT devices also introduce an array of vulnerabilities that threat actors can exploit.

Common IoT Device Vulnerabilities

IoT device vulnerabilities manifest in various forms and can result from design flaws, implementation errors, or inadequate security practices. Some of the most prevalent IoT device vulnerabilities include:

1.   **Lack of Encryption:** Many IoT devices transmit data without encryption, making it susceptible to interception and eavesdropping.

2.   **Insecure Authentication:** Weak or non-existent authentication mechanisms can allow unauthorized access to IoT devices, potentially compromising their functionality and data.

3.   **Default Credentials:** Manufacturers often ship

devices with default usernames and passwords that users may not change. Attackers can exploit these credentials to gain access.

4.   **Inadequate Firmware Security:** Firmware updates are essential for addressing security vulnerabilities. However, if firmware updates are not signed or validated, attackers can inject malicious firmware.

5.   **Lack of Regular Updates:** Some IoT devices lack mechanisms for receiving security patches or updates, leaving them vulnerable to known exploits.

6.   **Insecure APIs:** Insecure Application Programming Interfaces (APIs) can expose IoT devices to unauthorized control or data leakage.

7.   **Poor Physical Security:** Physical access to an IoT device can lead to tampering, data theft, or the insertion of malicious hardware.

8.   **Weak or Unsecured Communication Protocols:** The use of insecure communication protocols can facilitate eavesdropping and man-in-the-middle attacks.

9.   **Vendor-Specific Issues:** Some IoT devices may have unique vulnerabilities introduced during the manufacturing process or due to vendor-specific implementations.

Implications of IoT Device Vulnerabilities

The consequences of IoT device vulnerabilities can be severe and wide-ranging:

1. **Privacy Breaches:** Unauthorized access to IoT devices can compromise user privacy, exposing personal data, location information, and even audio/video feeds.

2. **Data Theft:** IoT devices often collect and transmit sensitive data. A breach can result in data theft, leading to identity theft, financial loss, or reputational damage.

3. **Malicious Control:** Attackers gaining control of IoT devices can manipulate their functions, potentially causing physical harm or disruptions.

4. **Botnets and DDoS Attacks:** Compromised IoT devices are often recruited into botnets and used for launching Distributed Denial of Service (DDoS) attacks on other targets.

5. **Unauthorized Surveillance:** IoT devices with cameras and microphones can be used for unauthorized surveillance or espionage.

Mitigation and Prevention

Addressing IoT device vulnerabilities requires a multifaceted approach:

1.   **Secure Design:** Manufacturers should prioritize security during the design phase, including encryption, secure authentication, and rigorous testing.

2.   **Regular Updates:** Provide a mechanism for firmware updates and encourage users to keep devices up to date.

3.   **Strong Authentication:** Implement strong authentication mechanisms, including multi-factor authentication (MFA) where possible.

4.   **Monitoring and Analytics:** Employ continuous monitoring and analytics to detect suspicious activity on IoT networks.

5.   **Network Segmentation:** Segment IoT devices from critical infrastructure to limit the potential impact of breaches.

6.   **Education and Awareness:** Educate both manufacturers and users about IoT security best practices and potential risks.

7.   **Compliance:** Encourage adherence to IoT security standards and regulatory requirements.

Conclusion

IoT device vulnerabilities underscore the importance of securing the rapidly expanding world of interconnected devices.

As the IoT ecosystem continues to evolve, vigilance, proactive security measures, and collaboration among manufacturers, users, and security experts are crucial to mitigating the risks associated with IoT device vulnerabilities. By addressing these vulnerabilities, we can harness the potential of IoT while minimizing the security challenges it presents.

D. Securing Mobile and IoT Devices: Safeguarding the Connected World

In an age dominated by the Internet of Things (IoT) and mobile devices, the world has grown more connected than ever before. Smartphones, tablets, wearables, and a vast array of IoT devices have become integral parts of our daily lives, bringing convenience and efficiency. However, this connectivity also introduces a host of security challenges, as these devices can become entry points for cyberattacks and data breaches. To navigate this complex landscape safely, securing mobile and IoT devices is paramount.

The Complexity of Mobile and IoT Security

Securing mobile and IoT devices is a multifaceted task, given the diversity of devices, operating systems, communication protocols, and usage scenarios. Whether it's a smartphone accessing sensitive corporate data or a smart thermostat controlling home climate, each device represents a potential entry point for attackers if not properly secured.

Key Security Considerations

To ensure the security of mobile and IoT devices, several critical considerations must be addressed:

1.   **Authentication and Access Control:**

•   Implement strong, multi-factor authentication (MFA) to ensure that only authorized users can access devices and data.

•   Employ robust access control mechanisms to limit permissions and privileges based on user roles.

2.   **Encryption:**

•   Encrypt data both at rest and during transmission to protect it from unauthorized access.

•   Utilize strong encryption algorithms and key management practices.

3.   **Firmware and Software Updates:**

•   Regularly update device firmware and software to patch vulnerabilities and enhance security.

•   Enable automated updates where possible to ensure timely protection.

4.   **Network Security:**

•   Secure Wi-Fi and Bluetooth connections by using strong encryption and avoiding open networks.

•   Segment IoT devices from critical networks to minimize the impact of breaches.

5.   **IoT Device Hardening:**

•   Disable unnecessary services and ports on IoT devices to reduce the attack surface.

•   Change default passwords and credentials to unique, strong ones.

6.   **IoT Ecosystem Security:**

•   Implement strong authentication and encryption for communication between IoT devices and their platforms or cloud services.

•   Monitor the IoT ecosystem for unusual activity and employ anomaly detection.

7.   **Physical Security:**

•   Protect devices physically by using locks, enclosures, or secure locations to prevent tampering or theft.

8. **User Education:**

•   Educate users about safe practices, such as avoiding public Wi-Fi for sensitive transactions and not clicking on suspicious links or downloading unknown apps.

Challenges in Mobile and IoT Security

Securing mobile and IoT devices is not without its challenges:

1.   **Diverse Ecosystem:** The vast diversity of devices, operating systems, and communication protocols complicates standardization and security management.

2.   **Resource Constraints:** IoT devices, especially sensors and low-power devices, may have limited computing resources and memory, making security implementations challenging.

3.   **Legacy Devices:** Many older IoT devices lack security features, making them vulnerable to attacks.

4.   **Privacy Concerns:** IoT devices can collect extensive data about users, raising privacy concerns. Proper data handling and user consent mechanisms are essential.

Best Practices for Mobile and IoT Security

To mitigate these challenges and secure mobile and IoT devices effectively, adhere to best practices:

1.   **Security by Design:** Incorporate security measures from the design phase of device development, considering threat modeling and risk assessments.

2.   **Regular Audits and Testing:** Conduct security audits, vulnerability assessments, and penetration testing regularly to identify and remediate weaknesses.

3.   **Patch Management:** Establish a process for timely patch management and updates for all devices and their components.

4.   **Secure Communication:** Use secure communication protocols, including VPNs for remote access to devices, and implement secure coding practices.

5.   **Incident Response:** Develop an incident response plan specific to mobile and IoT security incidents, outlining actions for containment, investigation, and recovery.

6.   **Compliance and Regulations:** Stay informed about relevant regulations and compliance requirements, ensuring adherence to privacy and security standards.

Conclusion

Securing mobile and IoT devices is an ongoing process that demands vigilance, collaboration, and proactive measures from device manufacturers, developers, organizations, and users alike.

As the interconnected world continues to evolve, the ability to secure these devices becomes increasingly critical for safeguarding sensitive data, maintaining privacy, and ensuring the reliability of the IoT ecosystem. By implementing robust security measures and staying informed about emerging threats, we can harness the full potential of mobile and IoT devices while mitigating the inherent security risks.

Chapter 10:

Social Engineering and Phishing

In the realm of cybersecurity, human psychology can be both a vulnerability and a powerful tool. Social engineering is a crafty and often deceptive approach to hacking that preys on the fundamental aspects of human behavior. It's a technique that doesn't rely on sophisticated code or complex algorithms but rather on the art of manipulation and persuasion. At the heart of social engineering lies phishing, a deceptive practice that has become one of the most prevalent and dangerous threats in the digital landscape.

The Art of Deception

Social engineering is the digital age's equivalent of classic con artistry, and it exploits our innate human traits, such as trust, curiosity, and the desire to help others. Attackers use various psychological tactics to manipulate individuals into revealing sensitive information, granting access to secure systems, or performing actions that compromise security.

Phishing: The Baited Hook

Phishing, a subset of social engineering, is the practice of luring individuals into clicking on malicious links, downloading infected files, or disclosing sensitive information through seemingly legitimate channels. These deceptive messages can arrive in the form of emails, text messages, or even phone calls, often impersonating trusted entities such as banks, government agencies, or familiar websites.

This chapter explores the intricate world of social engineering and phishing, shedding light on the psychology behind these tactics and the devastating impact they can have on individuals and organizations. We will delve into the various forms of social engineering attacks, dissect phishing techniques, and equip you with the knowledge to recognize and defend against these insidious threats.

Join us on a journey into the minds of cyber adversaries as we uncover the tactics and strategies they employ to manipulate the human element of cybersecurity. By understanding the inner workings of social engineering and phishing, you'll be better prepared to guard against these digital deceptions and protect yourself and your organization from falling victim to their snares.

A. Social Engineering Techniques: The Art of Digital Deception

Social engineering is a subversive and manipulative approach to cybersecurity that exploits human psychology rather than technical vulnerabilities. It relies on the clever use of psychological tactics to deceive individuals or organizations into divulging sensitive information, granting unauthorized access, or performing actions that compromise security. Understanding the various social engineering techniques is crucial for recognizing and defending against these deceptive attacks.

1. Pretexting:

- **Description:** Pretexting involves the creation of a fabricated scenario or pretext to manipulate a target into disclosing information or performing an action.

- **Example:** A pretexter might pose as a bank employee and call a target, claiming there is a discrepancy in their account and requesting personal information to verify their identity.

- **Mitigation:** Verify the identity of individuals or organizations making requests, especially if they involve sensitive information or financial transactions.

2. Phishing:

- **Description:** Phishing is one of the most common social engineering techniques and typically involves sending deceptive emails or messages that appear legitimate to trick recipients into revealing personal information, clicking on malicious links, or downloading infected files.

- **Example:** A phishing email might impersonate a well-known bank, asking the recipient to click on a link to update their account details on a fake website.

- **Mitigation:** Educate users about recognizing phishing attempts, use email filtering, and avoid clicking on suspicious links or downloading attachments from unknown sources.

3. Baiting:

- **Description:** Baiting involves enticing targets with something appealing, such as free software, music downloads, or discounts, to trick them into downloading malware or revealing information.

- **Example:** Attackers might offer free movie downloads that come bundled with malware, enticing users to download and execute the malicious file.

- **Mitigation:** Avoid downloading files or clicking on links from untrusted sources, and use reputable antivirus software.

4. Tailgating (Piggybacking):

- **Description:** Tailgating occurs when an attacker gains physical access to a secured area or system by following an authorized person without proper verification.

- **Example:** An attacker may hold the door open for an

employee and gain unauthorized access to a restricted area.

- **Mitigation:** Enforce strict access controls and require authentication for entry into secure areas.

5. Impersonation:

- **Description:** Impersonation involves pretending to be someone else, such as a coworker, IT technician, or delivery person, to gain access or trust.

- **Example:** An attacker might dress as a maintenance worker to gain access to an office building, posing as an authorized personnel.

- **Mitigation:** Verify the identity of individuals who request access or present themselves in person.

6. Quid Pro Quo:

- **Description:** In this technique, an attacker offers a benefit or service in exchange for information or access.

- **Example:** An attacker might call employees, posing as IT support, and offer quick fixes or software upgrades in exchange for login credentials.

- **Mitigation:** Encourage employees to verify the legitimacy of offers before providing any information or access.

7. Diversion Theft:

• **Description:** Diversion theft involves creating a diversion to distract victims while an accomplice carries out a theft or unauthorized access.

• **Example:** An attacker might call a company's front desk and create a distraction, such as a fake emergency, while another attacker enters the premises unnoticed.

• **Mitigation:** Train employees to remain vigilant and report suspicious activities, especially during distractions.

8. Pharming:

• **Description:** Pharming involves redirecting legitimate website traffic to a fraudulent website without the user's knowledge.

• **Example:** Attackers might manipulate DNS settings to redirect users attempting to access a banking website to a fake site where login credentials are stolen.

• **Mitigation:** Use secure and reputable DNS services and regularly monitor network traffic for anomalies.

Conclusion

Social engineering techniques are diverse and ever-evolving, making them a persistent and dangerous threat in the cybersecurity landscape. Recognizing these tactics and educating individuals and organizations about them are essential steps in mitigating the risks associated with social engineering attacks. By fostering a culture of security awareness and implementing robust authentication and verification practices, it is possible to defend against the artful deceptions of social engineers and protect sensitive information and assets from exploitation.

B. Phishing Attacks: The Art of Deception in the Digital Age

Phishing attacks represent one of the most prevalent and insidious cyber threats in the digital landscape. These attacks prey on human psychology and trust, aiming to deceive individuals or organizations into divulging sensitive information, such as login credentials, financial details, or personal data. Understanding the anatomy of phishing attacks, their various forms, and mitigation strategies is essential for safeguarding against this ever-evolving threat.

The Anatomy of a Phishing Attack

Phishing attacks are characterized by their deceptive nature, relying on social engineering techniques to manipulate victims. Here's a breakdown of the typical components of a phishing attack:

1.   **Bait:** Phishing attacks begin with enticing bait, which could be in the form of an email, message, or even a phone call. Attackers often impersonate trusted entities, such as banks, government agencies, or popular online services.

2.   **Deception:** The bait is carefully crafted to appear legitimate, often featuring convincing logos, formatting, and language. Attackers aim to deceive recipients into believing the communication is from a reputable source.

3.   **Lure:** Phishing attempts contain a call to action that entices victims to take specific steps, such as clicking on a link, downloading an attachment, or providing sensitive information.

4.   **Malicious Payload:** Clicking on a link or downloading an attachment may lead to the delivery of malware, which can compromise the victim's device or network.

5.   **Data Harvesting:** If victims fall for the deception and provide sensitive information, such as usernames, passwords, credit card numbers, or social security numbers, attackers harvest this data for malicious purposes.

Common Forms of Phishing Attacks

Phishing attacks come in various forms, each tailored to exploit specific vulnerabilities or preferences of potential victims. Some common types of phishing attacks include:

1.   **Email Phishing:** Attackers send deceptive emails containing malicious links or attachments. This is the most prevalent form of phishing.

2.   **Spear Phishing:** A targeted form of phishing where attackers customize their messages for specific individuals or organizations, often using information gathered from social media or other sources.

3.   **Vishing (Voice Phishing):** Attackers use phone calls to impersonate legitimate entities and convince victims to divulge information or take action.

4.   **Smishing (SMS Phishing):** Phishing attacks conducted via text messages, often directing victims to click on links or call specific numbers.

5.   **Pharming:** Attackers manipulate DNS settings to redirect users to fraudulent websites that mimic legitimate ones.

Mitigation Strategies

Defending against phishing attacks requires a combination of user education, technical safeguards, and vigilant practices. Here are some effective mitigation strategies:

1.   **User Education:** Train individuals to recognize phishing attempts, emphasizing the importance of skepticism and verifying the authenticity of communications.

2.   **Email Filtering:** Implement email filtering solutions that can identify and block phishing emails before they reach recipients' inboxes.

3.   **Two-Factor Authentication (2FA):** Encourage the use of 2FA to add an extra layer of security, even if login credentials are compromised.

4.   **HTTPS:** Ensure websites use HTTPS to encrypt data in transit and provide visual cues, such as padlock icons, to verify a site's legitimacy.

5.   **URL Inspection:** Hover over links in emails to preview the actual URL before clicking on them. Be cautious of shortened URLs.

6.   **Verification:** Contact the purported sender through official channels (phone, official website, or in-person) to confirm the authenticity of requests.

7.   **Security Updates:** Keep devices, browsers, and security software up to date to mitigate vulnerabilities that attackers may exploit.

8.   **Reporting:** Encourage users to report phishing attempts to IT or security teams for investigation and response.

Conclusion

Phishing attacks continue to evolve in sophistication and creativity, making them a persistent threat to individuals and organizations. By fostering a culture of security awareness, implementing technical safeguards, and staying vigilant, it is possible to reduce the risk of falling victim to these deceptive attacks. Recognizing the hallmarks of phishing attempts and maintaining a healthy level of skepticism are essential in defending against the artful deceptions of phishers and safeguarding sensitive information and assets from compromise.

C. Malware Delivery via Social Engineering: Exploiting Trust and Deception

Malware delivery through social engineering is a cunning and effective tactic employed by cybercriminals to infect devices and networks. It relies on manipulating human psychology and trust to deceive victims into inadvertently downloading or executing malicious software. Understanding how malware is delivered via social engineering is essential for recognizing and defending against these deceptive attacks.

The Art of Deception

Social engineering, including malware delivery, leverages psychological manipulation to achieve its objectives. In the context of malware delivery, attackers use tactics that deceive individuals into taking actions that compromise their devices and security.

Common Malware Delivery Techniques via Social Engineering

1. **Malicious Email Attachments:**

•   **Description:** Attackers send emails with seemingly innocuous attachments (e.g., PDFs, Word documents) that contain malware. These attachments often exploit vulnerabilities in software or rely on macros to execute malicious code.

•   **Example:** A victim receives an email with an attached PDF claiming to be an invoice. When opened, the PDF exploits a vulnerability to execute malware on the victim's device.

•   **Mitigation:** Be cautious when opening email attachments, especially from unknown or unverified sources. Keep software and applications up to date to patch vulnerabilities.

2. **Deceptive Links:**

•   **Description:** Attackers send emails or messages containing links to malicious websites. Victims are lured into clicking these links, which lead to drive-by downloads of malware.

- **Example:** An email appears to be from a legitimate service provider, asking the victim to click on a link to reset their password. Clicking the link directs the victim to a fake website that delivers malware.

- **Mitigation:** Hover over links to preview their actual destination before clicking. Ensure the website's URL matches the legitimate site.

3.   **Phishing Attachments:**

- **Description:** Phishing emails often include malicious attachments that impersonate trusted entities, such as banks or government agencies. Victims are prompted to open these attachments, leading to malware installation.

- **Example:** A phishing email mimics an official government notification and includes an attachment that, when opened, installs malware on the victim's device.

- **Mitigation:** Verify the authenticity of email senders and be cautious when downloading attachments, especially from unsolicited or suspicious sources.

4.   **Malvertising:**

- **Description:** Malvertisements are online ads containing malicious code. When users click on these ads or visit compromised websites, malware is delivered to their devices.

- **Example:** A seemingly legitimate online advertisement on a popular website contains malicious code. When clicked, the ad redirects users to a site that delivers malware.

- **Mitigation:** Use ad blockers and maintain up-to-date antivirus software. Avoid clicking on online ads, especially those that seem out of place.

Mitigation Strategies

Defending against malware delivery via social engineering requires a proactive approach:

1.   **User Education:** Educate users about the risks of social engineering attacks and train them to recognize suspicious emails, attachments, and links.

2.   **Email Filtering:** Implement email filtering solutions to detect and quarantine malicious emails and attachments.

3.   **Secure Browsing Practices:** Encourage users to be cautious when clicking on links and to verify the legitimacy of websites.

4.   **Patch and Update:** Regularly update operating systems, software, and applications to patch vulnerabilities that malware may exploit.

5.   **Security Software:** Use reputable antivirus and anti-

malware software to detect and remove malicious programs.

6.   **Least Privilege Access:** Limit user privileges to reduce the impact of malware if a device becomes infected.

7.   **Incident Response:** Develop an incident response plan to promptly address malware infections and minimize their impact.

Conclusion

Malware delivery via social engineering is a crafty and pervasive threat in the cybersecurity landscape. Cybercriminals adeptly exploit human psychology and trust to compromise devices and networks. By combining user education with technical safeguards and vigilant practices, individuals and organizations can reduce the risk of falling victim to these deceptive tactics. Recognizing the hallmarks of social engineering attacks and maintaining a security-conscious mindset are crucial in defending against malware delivery via social engineering and safeguarding sensitive information and systems from compromise.

D. Social Engineering Prevention: Strengthening the Human Firewall

Social engineering attacks, which exploit human psychology and trust to manipulate individuals or organizations, are among the most pervasive and deceptive cyber threats. Prevention is the first line of defense against these attacks, as it aims to reduce the susceptibility of individuals and organizations to social engineering tactics. Understanding and implementing effective prevention strategies is crucial for safeguarding against these cunning threats.

Building a Resilient Human Firewall

The term "human firewall" refers to the collective awareness and preparedness of individuals within an organization to defend against social engineering attacks. Preventing such attacks requires a combination of security measures, user education, and cultural changes.

Effective Social Engineering Prevention Strategies

1.   **Security Awareness Training:**

- **Description:** Regular and comprehensive security awareness training programs educate individuals about the tactics and techniques used in social engineering attacks. This empowers them to recognize and respond effectively to potential threats.

- **Benefits:** Users become more vigilant and cautious, reducing the likelihood of falling victim to social engineering schemes.

- **Implementation:** Conduct periodic training sessions,

phishing simulations, and provide resources for ongoing education.

2.   **Phishing Simulations:**

• **Description:** Phishing simulations involve sending fake phishing emails to employees to assess their susceptibility to such attacks. These simulations can help identify areas where additional training is needed.

• **Benefits:** Phishing simulations provide real-world testing of an organization's preparedness and help gauge the effectiveness of security awareness training.

• **Implementation:** Conduct regular phishing simulations and provide feedback and additional training based on the results.

3.   **Strong Authentication:**

• **Description:** Implement strong authentication mechanisms, such as multi-factor authentication (MFA), to add an extra layer of security. Even if attackers obtain usernames and passwords, MFA can prevent unauthorized access.

• **Benefits:** MFA mitigates the risk of unauthorized access, even in cases of credential theft through social engineering.

- **Implementation:** Require MFA for accessing sensitive systems and data.

4.   **Email Filtering:**

- **Description:** Employ email filtering solutions that can detect and block phishing emails before they reach users' inboxes.

- **Benefits:** Email filtering reduces the exposure to phishing attempts and prevents users from encountering deceptive messages.

- **Implementation:** Use advanced email filtering tools and keep them up to date.

5.   **Secure Browsing Practices:**

- **Description:** Encourage users to practice secure browsing by verifying website URLs, avoiding clicking on suspicious links or ads, and not downloading files from untrusted sources.

- **Benefits:** Secure browsing practices can prevent users from visiting malicious websites or falling for deceptive links.

- **Implementation:** Provide guidelines and training on secure browsing habits.

6.   **Incident Reporting:**

- **Description:** Establish clear procedures for reporting suspicious activities or potential security incidents. Encourage users to report any emails, messages, or interactions that seem suspicious.

- **Benefits:** Prompt reporting enables timely incident response and can prevent further social engineering attempts.

- **Implementation:** Educate users about the incident reporting process and provide accessible channels for reporting.

7.   **Culture of Security:**

- **Description:** Foster a culture of security within the organization, where security is viewed as everyone's responsibility. Encourage open communication about security issues and promote a sense of shared accountability.

- **Benefits:** A security-conscious culture promotes collective vigilance and proactive defense against social engineering.

- **Implementation:** Leadership should champion security initiatives and set an example of security-conscious behavior.

8.   **Regular Updates and Patch Management:**

•   **Description:** Keep software, operating systems, and applications up to date with the latest security patches to mitigate vulnerabilities that attackers may exploit.

•   **Benefits:** Regular updates minimize the risk of malware delivery and exploitation of software vulnerabilities.

•   **Implementation:** Establish a patch management process to ensure timely updates.

Conclusion

Preventing social engineering attacks requires a multifaceted approach that combines user education, technical safeguards, and a security-aware culture. By strengthening the human firewall, organizations can reduce their susceptibility to these deceptive tactics and enhance their overall cybersecurity posture. Recognizing the importance of social engineering prevention and fostering a security-conscious mindset are critical steps in defending against the artful deceptions of social engineers and safeguarding sensitive information and systems from compromise.

Chapter 11:

Network Security and Penetration Testing

In the ever-evolving landscape of cybersecurity, network security stands as the digital fortress protecting an organization's sensitive data and systems. To fortify these defenses, cybersecurity professionals employ a critical practice known as penetration testing, or "pen testing." This chapter delves into the realm of network security and explores the crucial role of penetration testing in identifying vulnerabilities, assessing security postures, and fortifying the digital perimeters that guard against cyber threats.

The Digital Perimeter: A Vulnerable Frontier

Networks serve as the digital arteries of organizations, facilitating communication, data sharing, and operations on an unprecedented scale. However, they also represent prime targets for malicious actors seeking to exploit vulnerabilities, gain unauthorized access, or compromise sensitive information. Network security is the art and science of safeguarding these interconnected systems from an array of threats, from cybercriminals and hackers to malware and data breaches.

The Role of Penetration Testing

Penetration testing is a systematic and controlled process of probing network systems, applications, and infrastructure for weaknesses. It simulates real-world attack scenarios, allowing cybersecurity professionals to uncover vulnerabilities before malicious actors do. This practice provides valuable insights into an organization's security posture, enabling proactive measures to mitigate risks and enhance defenses.

What to Expect in this Chapter

In the chapters that follow, we will embark on a comprehensive exploration of network security, delving into various aspects of securing digital ecosystems. Topics covered will include best practices in network security, the deployment of robust security policies, compliance with regulations, and the ever-evolving landscape of cyber threats.

Additionally, we will dive deep into the world of penetration testing, exploring methodologies, tools, and frameworks used by cybersecurity professionals to assess network vulnerabilities and bolster security. You will gain insights into how ethical hackers identify weaknesses, exploit them, and provide organizations with actionable recommendations to fortify their defenses.

Join us on this journey through the intricacies of network security and penetration testing. By understanding the principles and practices that underpin these critical disciplines, you'll be better equipped to defend against emerging cyber threats and ensure the resilience of your organization's digital infrastructure.

A. Network Security Best Practices: Safeguarding the Digital Perimeter

Network security is the foundation of an organization's cybersecurity posture, serving as the first line of defense against a myriad of cyber threats. Effective network security involves implementing a combination of strategies, policies, and technologies to protect digital assets, data, and communication channels. In this in-depth exploration, we'll uncover the essential network security best practices that organizations should follow to fortify their digital perimeters.

1. Network Segmentation:

- **Description:** Network segmentation involves dividing a network into smaller, isolated segments or subnetworks. This limits lateral movement for attackers and reduces the potential impact of a breach.

- **Benefits:** Segmentation enhances security by containing threats, improving network performance, and facilitating better access control.

- **Implementation:** Deploy firewalls, VLANs (Virtual

Local Area Networks), and access control lists (ACLs) to create network segments.

2. Access Control:

• **Description:** Access control mechanisms, such as firewalls, Intrusion Detection Systems (IDS), and Intrusion Prevention Systems (IPS), are used to restrict and monitor network traffic based on predefined policies.

• **Benefits:** Access control ensures that only authorized users and devices can access specific resources, reducing the risk of unauthorized access and data breaches.

• **Implementation:** Configure firewalls to permit only necessary traffic, implement strong authentication, and regularly review and update access policies.

3. Regular Patching and Updates:

• **Description:** Keeping network devices, operating systems, and software up to date with the latest security patches and updates is crucial to mitigate vulnerabilities.

• **Benefits:** Patch management reduces the risk of exploitation by attackers who target known vulnerabilities.

• **Implementation:** Establish a patch management process to identify, test, and apply patches in a timely manner.

4. Intrusion Detection and Prevention:

- **Description:** Intrusion Detection Systems (IDS) and Intrusion Prevention Systems (IPS) monitor network traffic for suspicious activity or known attack patterns. IDS alert administrators to potential threats, while IPS can block or mitigate attacks in real time.

- **Benefits:** IDS and IPS help identify and respond to threats promptly, preventing or minimizing damage.

- **Implementation:** Deploy IDS/IPS solutions and regularly update their threat detection signatures.

5. Network Monitoring and Logging:

- **Description:** Continuous network monitoring and robust logging practices provide visibility into network activities. Logs record events, errors, and anomalies, aiding in incident detection and response.

- **Benefits:** Monitoring and logging enable the early detection of security incidents, facilitate forensic analysis, and support compliance requirements.

- **Implementation:** Utilize network monitoring tools and ensure logs are securely stored and regularly reviewed.

6. Employee Training and Awareness:

- **Description:** Training employees about cybersecurity best practices and the risks associated with network security breaches is critical. Employees are often the first line of defense against social engineering attacks.

- **Benefits:** Educated employees are more likely to recognize and report security threats, reducing the success rate of attacks.

- **Implementation:** Conduct regular security awareness training sessions and simulate phishing attacks to test employee readiness.

7. Data Encryption:

- **Description:** Data encryption protects data in transit and at rest by converting it into unreadable ciphertext that can only be decrypted with the appropriate keys.

- **Benefits:** Encryption safeguards sensitive information from eavesdropping and unauthorized access.

- **Implementation:** Use encryption protocols (e.g., SSL/TLS for web traffic, VPNs for remote access) and encrypt sensitive data stored on servers or in databases.

8. Incident Response Plan:

- **Description:** Establishing an incident response plan is crucial for promptly detecting, mitigating, and recovering from security incidents. It outlines the steps to be taken when a breach occurs.

- **Benefits:** A well-defined incident response plan minimizes the impact of security incidents and helps maintain business continuity.

- **Implementation:** Develop and regularly test an incident response plan that includes roles, responsibilities, and communication procedures.

Conclusion

Network security best practices form the cornerstone of an organization's cybersecurity defenses. By implementing robust segmentation, access control, patch management, monitoring, and employee training, organizations can significantly reduce the risk of cyber threats and protect their digital assets. Staying vigilant, regularly updating security measures, and adapting to evolving threats are essential in maintaining a strong network security posture and safeguarding sensitive information and systems from compromise.

B. Penetration Testing Frameworks: Uncovering Vulnerabilities with Metasploit

Penetration testing is a critical component of cybersecurity, allowing organizations to proactively identify and remediate vulnerabilities in their digital infrastructure. Penetration testing frameworks like Metasploit have become invaluable tools for ethical hackers and security professionals. In this in-depth exploration, we'll delve into the world of penetration testing frameworks, with a focus on Metasploit, to understand how they are used to assess and strengthen an organization's security posture.

Understanding Penetration Testing Frameworks

Penetration testing frameworks are comprehensive toolkits designed to assist security professionals in identifying and exploiting vulnerabilities within computer systems, networks, and applications. These frameworks facilitate the ethical hacking process by providing a wide range of tools, scripts, and exploits that can be used to simulate real-world cyberattacks. They help security teams uncover weaknesses in their defenses before malicious actors do, allowing for timely remediation.

Metasploit: An Overview

Metasploit is perhaps the most renowned and widely used penetration testing framework. It was developed by Rapid7 and is available in both open-source (Metasploit Framework) and commercial versions (Metasploit Pro). Metasploit has gained popularity due to its versatility, extensive exploit database, and active user community.

Key Components of Metasploit:

1.   **Framework:** The core of Metasploit provides a powerful interface for managing and launching exploits, payloads, and auxiliary modules. It allows users to organize and track their penetration testing activities.

2.   **Exploits:** Metasploit includes a vast repository of exploits for known vulnerabilities in various operating systems, applications, and devices. These exploits are prepackaged and can be readily used during testing.

3.   **Payloads:** Payloads are pieces of code that are delivered to a target system after a successful exploit. They provide the attacker with various functionalities, such as remote access, data exfiltration, or system manipulation.

4.   **Auxiliary Modules:** Auxiliary modules are non-exploitative tools that serve various functions, including scanning, fingerprinting, and information gathering. They are invaluable for reconnaissance and initial assessments.

5.   **Post-Exploitation Modules:** Once a system is compromised, Metasploit offers post-exploitation modules that

help security professionals maintain access, gather information, and perform additional actions on the target system.

How Metasploit is Used:

1.   **Reconnaissance:** Security professionals use Metasploit for initial reconnaissance, identifying potential targets and vulnerabilities.

2.   **Scanning and Enumeration:** Metasploit provides tools for scanning and enumerating target systems to gather information about open ports, services, and potential vulnerabilities.

3.   **Exploitation:** Once vulnerabilities are identified, Metasploit can be used to launch exploits, gaining access to target systems.

4.   **Post-Exploitation:** After successful exploitation, security professionals can use Metasploit to maintain access, escalate privileges, and gather sensitive information from compromised systems.

5.   **Reporting:** Metasploit assists in generating detailed reports, documenting vulnerabilities, exploited systems, and remediation recommendations.

Ethical Use and Legal Considerations:

It's important to emphasize that Metasploit and other penetration testing frameworks should be used ethically and in compliance with applicable laws and regulations. Unauthorized penetration testing can lead to legal consequences. Organizations should ensure that they have explicit permission to conduct penetration tests and should follow established guidelines and reporting procedures.

Conclusion

Penetration testing frameworks like Metasploit are invaluable tools for ethical hackers and security professionals. They play a crucial role in assessing an organization's security posture, identifying vulnerabilities, and aiding in remediation efforts. When used responsibly and in adherence to ethical guidelines and legal considerations, these frameworks contribute to a stronger cybersecurity defense, helping organizations protect their sensitive data and systems from real-world threats.

C. Reporting and Remediation in Cybersecurity: Closing the Gap Between Vulnerabilities and Security

In the complex landscape of cybersecurity, reporting and remediation represent the critical bridge between identifying vulnerabilities and bolstering an organization's security posture. This in-depth exploration will uncover the significance of reporting and remediation processes, highlighting their essential roles in managing and mitigating security risks effectively.

The Cybersecurity Paradox

As the digital realm becomes increasingly intertwined with everyday life and business operations, cybersecurity threats continue to proliferate. Cybercriminals are continually evolving their tactics, making it more challenging than ever for organizations to stay one step ahead. This escalating threat landscape underscores the importance of robust reporting and remediation practices.

Reporting Vulnerabilities: The First Step

Reporting vulnerabilities is the initial step in the cybersecurity lifecycle. It involves the identification and documentation of security weaknesses within an organization's digital infrastructure, including systems, networks, applications, and data. Key aspects of this process include:

1.   **Discovery:** Vulnerabilities can be discovered through various means, including security assessments, penetration testing, monitoring, and incident response. Prompt discovery is crucial to minimize exposure to potential threats.

2.   **Assessment:** Once identified, vulnerabilities are assessed for their severity, potential impact, and the likelihood of exploitation. This assessment helps prioritize remediation efforts.

3.   **Documentation:** Comprehensive documentation is essential, including details about the vulnerability, its location, affected systems, and evidence of its existence. Accurate records aid in tracking and remediation.

4.   **Classification:** Vulnerabilities are typically categorized based on their severity, using a common scale such as the Common Vulnerability Scoring System (CVSS). This classification guides remediation prioritization.

Remediation: Closing the Security Gap

Remediation is the process of addressing and resolving identified vulnerabilities to enhance an organization's security posture. It is a proactive and strategic effort aimed at reducing the attack surface and minimizing potential risks. Key aspects of the remediation process include:

1.   **Prioritization:** Not all vulnerabilities are equal in terms of risk. Prioritization is critical, and organizations should focus on addressing the most critical and exploitable vulnerabilities first.

2.   **Patch Management:** One common method of

remediation involves applying security patches and updates to vulnerable systems, software, and devices. Regular patching helps close known security gaps.

3.   **Configuration Management:** Proper configuration management involves securing systems by configuring them according to industry best practices and security guidelines.

4.   **Implementing Security Controls:** Additional security controls, such as firewalls, intrusion detection systems, and access controls, can be deployed to mitigate vulnerabilities and enhance security.

5.   **Testing:** Post-remediation testing is essential to verify that vulnerabilities have been effectively addressed and that the changes made during remediation do not introduce new vulnerabilities.

6.   **Monitoring:** Continuous monitoring is crucial to ensure that vulnerabilities do not resurface and that the security posture remains robust over time.

Reporting: Communication and Accountability

Reporting vulnerabilities and remediation efforts is more than just a procedural requirement; it is a vital component of a transparent and accountable cybersecurity program. Reporting serves several crucial purposes:

1.   **Communication:** Reporting ensures that all relevant stakeholders, including IT teams, security teams, management, and even external partners, are aware of vulnerabilities and their status.

2.   **Accountability:** Reporting holds individuals and teams accountable for addressing vulnerabilities and achieving remediation goals.

3.   **Decision-Making:** Reports provide decision-makers with the necessary information to allocate resources, set priorities, and make informed choices regarding cybersecurity investments.

4.   **Compliance:** Reporting is often a compliance requirement, ensuring that organizations adhere to industry regulations and standards.

5.   **Continuous Improvement:** By analyzing reporting data, organizations can identify recurring issues, assess the effectiveness of remediation efforts, and refine their cybersecurity strategies.

Conclusion

Reporting and remediation are fundamental pillars of cybersecurity, serving as the linchpin between vulnerability discovery and a robust security posture. The ever-evolving threat landscape necessitates a proactive approach to identifying vulnerabilities, assessing their impact, and swiftly remediating them. By fostering a culture of transparency, accountability, and continuous improvement, organizations can effectively manage cybersecurity risks, protect sensitive data, and fortify their defenses against an array of cyber threats.

D. Compliance and Regulations in Cybersecurity: Navigating the Complex Regulatory Landscape

In the interconnected digital world, cybersecurity is not just a matter of best practices; it is also heavily influenced by compliance and regulations. In this in-depth exploration, we will uncover the intricate relationship between compliance, regulations, and cybersecurity, and how organizations navigate this complex landscape to protect sensitive data, ensure privacy, and meet legal requirements.

The Regulatory Landscape

The regulatory landscape for cybersecurity is vast and continually evolving. Governments, industry bodies, and international organizations have established a multitude of rules and regulations to address the growing threats in cyberspace. Key elements of this landscape include:

1.   **Industry-Specific Regulations:** Various industries,

such as finance, healthcare, and energy, have their own cybersecurity regulations tailored to the unique risks and challenges they face. For example, the Health Insurance Portability and Accountability Act (HIPAA) governs healthcare data security, while the Payment Card Industry Data Security Standard (PCI DSS) applies to the financial sector.

2.   **International Regulations:** In an era of global data flows, international regulations like the European Union's General Data Protection Regulation (GDPR) and the California Consumer Privacy Act (CCPA) have far-reaching implications. These regulations aim to protect individuals' privacy rights and impose strict requirements on how organizations handle personal data.

3.   **Government Initiatives:** Many governments have introduced national cybersecurity initiatives and regulations. In the United States, the Federal Information Security Modernization Act (FISMA) mandates cybersecurity standards for federal agencies. Similarly, the Cybersecurity Maturity Model Certification (CMMC) is emerging as a requirement for defense contractors.

4.   **Data Breach Notification Laws:** Numerous regions have enacted data breach notification laws, which require organizations to notify affected individuals and authorities when a breach involving sensitive data occurs. Failure to comply can result in significant penalties.

The Role of Compliance in Cybersecurity

Compliance refers to an organization's adherence to the regulations and standards applicable to its industry and geographic location. Compliance is not just about avoiding legal trouble; it is about establishing a robust security posture that protects sensitive information. Key aspects of compliance in cybersecurity include:

1.   **Risk Assessment:** Compliance often begins with a risk assessment to identify vulnerabilities and threats. Organizations must assess their security controls, data handling practices, and potential risks to determine where compliance gaps exist.

2.   **Security Controls:** Compliance standards typically outline specific security controls that organizations must implement. These controls may include access controls, encryption, monitoring, and incident response procedures.

3.   **Documentation:** Compliance requires thorough documentation of security policies, procedures, and practices. Proper documentation helps demonstrate compliance to auditors and regulators.

4.   **Auditing and Assessment:** Many compliance frameworks require regular auditing and assessment of an organization's cybersecurity practices. These assessments help verify that controls are effective and that compliance requirements are met.

5. **Incident Response:** Compliance often includes requirements for incident response planning and reporting. Organizations must have procedures in place to detect, report, and remediate security incidents.

Challenges of Compliance

While compliance is essential for ensuring cybersecurity and protecting sensitive data, it comes with its own set of challenges:

1. **Complexity:** Navigating the myriad of compliance regulations and standards can be overwhelming. Organizations must determine which regulations apply to them and understand the specific requirements of each.

2. **Resource Intensity:** Achieving and maintaining compliance can be resource-intensive. It requires dedicated staff, budget allocations, and ongoing efforts to keep pace with changing regulations.

3. **Consistency:** Ensuring that compliance measures are consistently implemented across an organization, especially in large enterprises, can be a significant challenge.

4. **Evolving Threat Landscape:** Regulations and compliance frameworks may struggle to keep up with the rapidly evolving threat landscape. Cybersecurity threats often outpace regulatory updates.

Benefits of Compliance

Despite the challenges, compliance offers several benefits:

1.   **Data Protection:** Compliance regulations are designed to protect sensitive data and personal information. Compliant organizations are better equipped to safeguard customer and employee data.

2.   **Reputation Management:** Compliance helps build trust with customers and partners. Being compliant demonstrates a commitment to security and privacy, enhancing an organization's reputation.

3.   **Legal Protection:** Compliance helps organizations avoid legal trouble and financial penalties. It provides a legal framework for addressing data breaches and other cybersecurity incidents.

4.   **Competitive Advantage:** Compliance can be a competitive advantage, especially when seeking contracts or partnerships with organizations that prioritize cybersecurity.

Conclusion

Compliance and regulations play an integral role in shaping cybersecurity practices, protecting data, and ensuring privacy. Organizations must navigate a complex landscape of industry-specific, international, and government regulations while continuously adapting to the evolving threat landscape. Compliance not only minimizes legal risks but also promotes a robust cybersecurity culture that safeguards sensitive information and enhances an organization's reputation in an increasingly connected world.

Chapter 12:

Advanced Ethical Hacking Topics

As the cybersecurity landscape continues to evolve, so do the skills and knowledge required of ethical hackers. In this chapter, we embark on a journey into the realm of advanced ethical hacking topics. Building on the foundations of ethical hacking, we delve deeper into the intricacies of cyber threats, defense strategies, and cutting-edge techniques employed by security professionals to protect digital assets and thwart malicious actors.

The Constant Evolution of Cyber Threats

In the ever-evolving cyber threat landscape, hackers are continually refining their tactics, developing new attack vectors, and exploiting vulnerabilities with unprecedented sophistication. To effectively counter these threats, ethical hackers must stay one step ahead, mastering advanced techniques and tools that can uncover hidden vulnerabilities, detect elusive threats, and strengthen cyber defenses.

What to Expect in this Chapter

Throughout this chapter, we will explore a diverse array of advanced ethical hacking topics, including:

1. **Advanced Persistent Threats (APTs):** These insidious and highly targeted attacks represent a pinnacle of cyber threat sophistication. We will delve into the anatomy of APTs, their strategies, and how ethical hackers can detect and respond to these stealthy adversaries.

2. **Cloud Security Testing:** As organizations increasingly migrate to cloud environments, understanding the nuances of cloud security becomes paramount. We will explore the unique challenges and strategies for securing cloud-based assets.

3. **Red Team vs. Blue Team Exercises:** Simulation-based training exercises pit "Red Teams" (offensive security professionals) against "Blue Teams" (defensive security teams) to enhance an organization's security posture. We will delve into the world of red teaming, blue teaming, and how these exercises contribute to robust cyber defenses.

4. **Hacking for Bug Bounties:** Ethical hackers often participate in bug bounty programs, helping organizations identify and patch vulnerabilities in exchange for rewards. We will explore the mechanics of bug bounty programs and the ethical hacking skills required to excel in this field.

5. **Ethical Hacking in Industrial Control Systems (ICS):** Industrial environments, including critical infrastructure, are increasingly becoming targets for cyberattacks. We will

investigate the unique challenges and ethical hacking approaches to securing ICS.

These advanced topics represent the cutting edge of ethical hacking practices, providing security professionals with the insights and tools needed to safeguard digital ecosystems against the most sophisticated cyber threats.

Join us on this exploration of advanced ethical hacking topics, where we uncover the strategies, techniques, and ethical considerations that underpin the evolving field of cybersecurity. By mastering these advanced concepts, ethical hackers can play a pivotal role in fortifying defenses, safeguarding critical systems, and protecting digital assets in an era of relentless cyber threats.

A. Advanced Persistent Threats (APTs): The Stealthy Adversaries of the Digital Age

In the ever-evolving landscape of cybersecurity, Advanced Persistent Threats (APTs) represent the pinnacle of sophistication and persistence in cyberattacks. APTs are highly targeted, well-funded, and often state-sponsored campaigns that pose a grave threat to governments, organizations, and critical infrastructure. In this comprehensive exploration, we will delve into the intricacies of APTs, understanding their characteristics, tactics, detection, and mitigation strategies.

Defining Advanced Persistent Threats (APTs)

Advanced Persistent Threats are long-term, covert, and highly focused cyberattacks orchestrated by skilled and resourceful threat actors. APTs are characterized by several key attributes:

1.   **Persistence:** APTs are not opportunistic. They demonstrate a sustained and patient approach, often extending over months or even years. Attackers maintain their presence within the target environment without raising suspicion.

2.   **Stealth:** APTs are designed to remain hidden from traditional security mechanisms. Attackers use sophisticated techniques to evade detection, including custom malware, zero-day exploits, and advanced evasion tactics.

3.   **Targeted:** APTs are highly targeted, focusing on specific organizations, industries, or even individuals. Threat actors invest significant time and effort in reconnaissance to gather intelligence about their targets.

4.   **Custom Tools:** APTs frequently employ custom-made tools and malware tailored to their specific objectives and targets. These tools are less likely to be detected by off-the-shelf security solutions.

5.   **Persistence and Control:** Once inside a target network, APT actors establish multiple points of persistence,

ensuring continued access and control. They move laterally through the network to achieve their objectives.

6.　　**Data Exfiltration:** A primary goal of APTs is to steal sensitive data, whether it's intellectual property, financial information, or government secrets. Data exfiltration is often carried out meticulously and covertly.

Stages of an APT Attack

APTs typically follow a series of stages during their lifecycle:

1.　　**Reconnaissance:** APT actors conduct extensive reconnaissance to identify potential targets, vulnerabilities, and entry points into the target organization. This may involve social engineering, open-source intelligence (OSINT) gathering, and scanning for weaknesses.

2.　　**Initial Compromise:** APTs gain an initial foothold in the target environment through techniques like spear-phishing, exploiting software vulnerabilities, or compromising supply chains.

3.　　**Establishing Persistence:** Once inside, APT actors establish multiple entry points and persistence mechanisms to maintain access even if one point is discovered and remediated.

4.　　**Lateral Movement:** APTs move laterally through the network, escalating privileges and seeking valuable assets. They often mimic legitimate user behavior to evade detection.

5.   **Data Exfiltration:** APTs carefully exfiltrate sensitive data, often compressing and encrypting it before sending it to external servers under their control.

Detecting and Mitigating APTs

Detecting and mitigating APTs require a multifaceted approach:

1.   **Anomaly Detection:** Implement advanced security analytics and anomaly detection systems to identify unusual or suspicious behavior within the network.

2.   **Threat Intelligence:** Stay informed about the latest APT campaigns and tactics through threat intelligence feeds. This knowledge can help organizations proactively defend against emerging threats.

3.   **Network Segmentation:** Segmenting the network can limit the lateral movement of APTs, containing them within isolated segments and minimizing their impact.

4.   **Zero Trust Security:** Adopt a "Zero Trust" security model, where no one is trusted by default, and strict access controls are enforced based on continuous authentication and authorization.

5.   **Incident Response:** Develop a robust incident response plan that includes procedures for APT detection, containment, eradication, and recovery.

6.   **User Education:** Train employees to recognize social engineering tactics and phishing attempts, as many APTs begin with targeted spear-phishing attacks.

7.   **Advanced Threat Hunting:** Invest in threat hunting teams that actively seek out signs of APT activity within the network.

Conclusion

Advanced Persistent Threats (APTs) represent a significant challenge in modern cybersecurity due to their stealth, persistence, and targeting of high-value assets. Organizations must adopt proactive, multi-layered security measures, invest in threat detection and response capabilities, and stay vigilant against emerging threats. By understanding the characteristics and tactics of APTs, security professionals can better defend against these sophisticated adversaries and protect sensitive data and systems from compromise.

B. Cloud Security Testing: Ensuring the Resilience of Cloud Environments

As organizations increasingly migrate their IT infrastructure and services to cloud environments, ensuring the security of cloud-based assets becomes paramount. Cloud security testing is a critical component of this strategy, designed to identify vulnerabilities, assess configurations, and strengthen the security posture of cloud deployments. In this comprehensive exploration, we will delve into the intricacies of cloud security testing, its significance, methodologies, and best practices.

The Significance of Cloud Security Testing

Cloud computing offers numerous benefits, including scalability, flexibility, and cost-efficiency. However, it also introduces unique security challenges. Cloud environments, whether public, private, or hybrid, host a wealth of sensitive data and critical applications. As such, they have become prime targets for cyberattacks. The significance of cloud security testing lies in:

1.   **Identifying Vulnerabilities:** Cloud security testing helps uncover vulnerabilities, misconfigurations, and weak points within cloud infrastructure, preventing potential exploitation by malicious actors.

2.   **Compliance:** Many industries and regulatory bodies require adherence to specific security standards. Cloud security testing assists in demonstrating compliance with these standards.

3.   **Risk Mitigation:** By proactively identifying and mitigating security risks, organizations reduce the likelihood of

data breaches, downtime, and reputational damage.

4.   **Data Protection:** Ensuring the security of data stored in the cloud is paramount. Cloud security testing helps safeguard sensitive information.

Methodologies of Cloud Security Testing

Effective cloud security testing encompasses various methodologies and approaches:

1.   **Vulnerability Scanning:** Automated scanning tools are used to identify known vulnerabilities in cloud assets. These scans cover operating systems, applications, and services.

2.   **Penetration Testing:** Ethical hackers simulate real-world cyberattacks to identify vulnerabilities that automated tools may miss. They test the effectiveness of security controls, authentication mechanisms, and network segmentation.

3.   **Configuration Assessment:** Ensuring that cloud configurations align with security best practices is crucial. Assessing configurations helps detect misconfigurations that could lead to data exposure.

4.   **Compliance Auditing:** Organizations must adhere to industry-specific compliance standards. Auditing cloud environments against these standards ensures that regulatory requirements are met.

5.   **Data Encryption Analysis:** Examining data encryption practices ensures that data in transit and at rest is appropriately protected.

6.   **Identity and Access Management (IAM) Review:** Verifying that IAM policies are correctly configured and that user access is restricted to the principle of least privilege helps prevent unauthorized access.

7.   **Incident Response Testing:** Simulating incident scenarios within the cloud environment helps assess an organization's readiness to respond to security incidents effectively.

Best Practices in Cloud Security Testing

1.   **Continuous Testing:** Security testing should be an ongoing process, adapting to changes in the cloud environment and the evolving threat landscape.

2.   **Collaboration:** Ensure collaboration between development, operations, and security teams to integrate security throughout the cloud deployment lifecycle.

3.   **Automated Testing:** Implement automated testing wherever possible to detect vulnerabilities quickly and consistently.

4.   **Documentation:**   Maintain   comprehensive

documentation of cloud security testing activities, findings, and remediation efforts.

5. **Third-Party Assessments:** Engage third-party security experts for independent assessments to gain an objective perspective on your cloud security.

6. **Education and Training:** Invest in training for your teams to stay updated with cloud security best practices and emerging threats.

Conclusion

Cloud security testing is an indispensable practice in safeguarding cloud-based assets against evolving cyber threats. As organizations increasingly rely on cloud services and infrastructure, they must ensure the resilience of their cloud environments. By adopting robust methodologies, best practices, and a continuous testing mindset, organizations can proactively identify and remediate vulnerabilities, bolster their cloud security posture, and embrace the benefits of cloud computing with confidence.

C. Red Team vs. Blue Team Exercises: Forging Strong Cybersecurity Through Adversarial Simulation

In the ever-evolving landscape of cybersecurity, organizations face a constant battle to protect their digital assets and data from an increasingly sophisticated array of threats. Red Team vs. Blue Team exercises represent a proactive and collaborative approach to fortifying defenses, enhancing incident response, and fostering a culture of continuous improvement. In this comprehensive exploration, we will delve into the intricacies of Red Team vs. Blue Team exercises, their significance, methodologies, and benefits.

Defining Red Team vs. Blue Team Exercises

Red Team vs. Blue Team exercises are simulated cybersecurity assessments that involve two opposing teams: the "Red Team" and the "Blue Team." Each team plays a distinct role:

- **Red Team:** The Red Team, also known as the "offensive" team, acts as the adversary. Its mission is to simulate cyberattacks, emulate the tactics, techniques, and procedures (TTPs) of real-world threat actors, and identify vulnerabilities and weaknesses within an organization's security infrastructure.

- **Blue Team:** The Blue Team, also known as the "defensive" team, is responsible for protecting the organization's assets and networks. Their role is to detect, respond to, and mitigate the simulated attacks launched by the Red Team. They also focus on strengthening security controls and practices.

The Significance of Red Team vs. Blue Team Exercises

These exercises serve several critical purposes:

1.   **Realistic Assessment:** Red Team vs. Blue Team exercises replicate real-world cyber threats, providing organizations with a realistic assessment of their security posture.

2.   **Continuous Improvement:** By exposing vulnerabilities and testing incident response capabilities, organizations can identify areas for improvement and refine their cybersecurity strategies.

3.   **Enhanced Security Awareness:** These exercises raise security awareness among employees and demonstrate the importance of adhering to security policies and best practices.

4.   **Incident Response Training:** Blue Teams gain valuable experience in responding to cyber incidents, reducing response times and minimizing potential damage during actual incidents.

Methodologies of Red Team vs. Blue Team Exercises

Effective Red Team vs. Blue Team exercises involve several key methodologies:

1.   **Scenario Development:** Exercises begin with the creation of realistic scenarios, such as simulating a ransomware

attack, data breach, or advanced persistent threat (APT) infiltration.

2.   **Rules of Engagement (ROE):** Clearly defined ROE outline the scope, objectives, and limitations of the exercise, ensuring a controlled and safe environment.

3.   **Adversarial Tactics:** The Red Team employs various tactics, such as social engineering, phishing, vulnerability exploitation, and penetration testing, to simulate cyberattacks.

4.   **Monitoring and Detection:** Blue Teams use monitoring tools, security information and event management (SIEM) systems, and intrusion detection systems (IDS) to detect Red Team activities.

5.   **Incident Response:** When the Blue Team identifies Red Team actions, they respond by containing, mitigating, and eradicating the threat, while also documenting the incident.

6.   **Debrief and Analysis:** After the exercise, both teams participate in a debriefing session to discuss findings, lessons learned, and areas for improvement.

Benefits of Red Team vs. Blue Team Exercises

1.   **Risk Mitigation:** These exercises help organizations proactively identify vulnerabilities and weaknesses before real cyber threats exploit them.

2. **Security Culture:** They promote a security-conscious culture, emphasizing the importance of vigilance and adherence to security protocols.

3. **Skill Development:** Red Team vs. Blue Team exercises enhance the skills of security professionals, making them more effective in defending against cyber threats.

4. **Incident Preparedness:** Blue Teams gain valuable experience in incident response, ensuring a more effective and coordinated response during actual incidents.

5. **Continuous Improvement:** Organizations use exercise findings to refine security policies, procedures, and technology investments continually.

Conclusion

Red Team vs. Blue Team exercises are invaluable tools for organizations seeking to bolster their cybersecurity defenses, train their security teams, and proactively identify and mitigate vulnerabilities. In a rapidly evolving threat landscape, these exercises enable organizations to stay one step ahead of adversaries by simulating realistic cyberattacks and continuously improving their security posture. By fostering collaboration between offensive and defensive teams, organizations can better protect their digital assets and data in an era of relentless cyber threats.

D. Hacking for Bug Bounties: Bridging the Gap Between Ethical Hacking and Cybersecurity Rewards

In the dynamic world of cybersecurity, organizations are increasingly turning to the global ethical hacking community to help identify and remediate vulnerabilities in their digital ecosystems. Bug bounty programs, which offer rewards to security researchers and ethical hackers for discovering and responsibly disclosing security flaws, have gained immense popularity. In this comprehensive exploration, we will delve into the intricacies of hacking for bug bounties, its significance, methodologies, and the symbiotic relationship it establishes between hackers and organizations.

Defining Bug Bounty Programs

Bug bounty programs are initiatives launched by organizations to incentivize external security researchers and ethical hackers to discover, report, and help mitigate security vulnerabilities in their systems, applications, and digital assets. These programs are a proactive and collaborative approach to identifying weaknesses before malicious actors can exploit them.

The Significance of Bug Bounty Programs

Bug bounty programs offer several significant benefits:

1.   **Enhanced Security:** By harnessing the collective

knowledge and expertise of a global community of ethical hackers, organizations can uncover vulnerabilities that may have gone unnoticed through traditional security measures.

2.   **Cost-Efficiency:** Bug bounty programs offer a cost-effective way to identify and fix vulnerabilities. Organizations pay only for valid vulnerabilities discovered, avoiding fixed labor costs associated with in-house security teams.

3.   **Continuous Improvement:** These programs encourage a culture of continuous improvement in an organization's security posture, as they must stay responsive to new vulnerabilities discovered by ethical hackers.

4.   **Reputation Enhancement:** Organizations that run successful bug bounty programs demonstrate a commitment to security and foster goodwill within the cybersecurity community, enhancing their reputation.

5.   **Legal and Ethical Disclosure:** Bug bounty programs provide a clear and ethical channel for security researchers to disclose vulnerabilities, reducing the risk of accidental or malicious exposure.

Methodologies of Hacking for Bug Bounties

Engaging in hacking for bug bounties involves a systematic approach:

1.   **Program Selection:** Ethical hackers choose a bug bounty program based on their interests, expertise, and the program's scope, rewards, and rules.

2.   **Reconnaissance:** Researchers gather information about the target, such as its assets, attack surfaces, and known vulnerabilities.

3.   **Testing and Exploitation:** Ethical hackers employ various tools and techniques to test for vulnerabilities, such as web application testing, network scanning, and vulnerability analysis.

4.   **Reporting:** When a vulnerability is discovered, the hacker submits a detailed report to the organization, including proof of concept, potential impact, and suggested mitigation.

5.   **Communication:** Effective communication with the organization's security team is crucial to ensure clear understanding and collaboration in resolving the issue.

6.   **Verification:** The organization's security team validates the reported vulnerability, often using a controlled environment to reproduce the findings.

7.   **Rewards and Recognition:** If the vulnerability is confirmed, the hacker is eligible for a reward, which can range from a nominal sum to substantial payouts depending on the severity and impact of the vulnerability.

Best Practices in Hacking for Bug Bounties

1.   **Responsible Disclosure:** Ethical hackers adhere to responsible disclosure guidelines, ensuring that vulnerabilities are reported promptly and that they do not exploit or share vulnerabilities publicly until they are patched.

2.   **Collaboration:** Maintaining open and transparent communication with the organization's security team is vital for successful collaboration.

3.   **Legal and Ethical Conduct:** Researchers must abide by ethical and legal standards, respecting the organization's terms and policies.

4.   **Continuous Learning:** Ethical hackers must stay up-to-date with the latest security trends, techniques, and vulnerabilities to remain effective in bug hunting.

Conclusion

Hacking for bug bounties represents a symbiotic relationship between ethical hackers and organizations, where security researchers actively contribute to improving an organization's cybersecurity while being rewarded for their efforts. Bug bounty programs have become an integral component of modern cybersecurity, promoting collaboration, transparency, and the continuous enhancement of security practices. By harnessing the skills and knowledge of the global ethical hacking community, organizations can strengthen their defenses and proactively identify and remediate vulnerabilities in an ever-evolving threat landscape.

E. Ethical Hacking in Industrial Control Systems (ICS): Protecting Critical Infrastructure in the Digital Age

Industrial Control Systems (ICS) play a pivotal role in managing and controlling critical infrastructure such as power plants, water treatment facilities, manufacturing plants, and transportation systems. As these systems become increasingly interconnected and digitized, they face a growing array of cyber threats. Ethical hacking in ICS, also known as "white hat" hacking, is a proactive approach to identifying and mitigating vulnerabilities in these systems while safeguarding the functioning of critical infrastructure. In this comprehensive exploration, we will delve into the intricacies of ethical hacking in ICS, its significance, methodologies, and the critical role it plays in maintaining the security and reliability of essential services.

Defining Industrial Control Systems (ICS)

Industrial Control Systems are specialized computer-based systems that monitor and control industrial processes. They consist of three primary components:

1.   **Supervisory Control and Data Acquisition (SCADA) Systems:** These systems gather and transmit real-time data from various sensors and devices, enabling operators to monitor and control industrial processes.

2.   **Distributed Control Systems (DCS):** DCS systems manage complex industrial processes and are responsible for precise control of machinery and equipment.

3.   **Programmable Logic Controllers (PLCs):** PLCs are specialized microcontrollers that automate processes based on pre-programmed logic, making them a crucial component of ICS.

The Significance of Ethical Hacking in ICS

The significance of ethical hacking in ICS lies in its role in safeguarding critical infrastructure:

1.   **Identification of Vulnerabilities:** Ethical hackers help identify vulnerabilities in ICS components, ensuring that potential weaknesses are discovered and remediated before they can be exploited by malicious actors.

2.   **Prevention of Disruptions:** By proactively addressing vulnerabilities, ethical hacking helps prevent cyber incidents that could disrupt essential services and have far-reaching consequences.

3.   **Compliance:** Many industries and regulatory bodies

require adherence to specific security standards for critical infrastructure. Ethical hacking ensures compliance with these standards.

4.   **Risk Mitigation:** Identifying and addressing vulnerabilities reduces the risk of data breaches, equipment damage, and operational disruptions in ICS environments.

Methodologies of Ethical Hacking in ICS

Effective ethical hacking in ICS involves several key methodologies:

1.   **Reconnaissance:** Ethical hackers gather information about the ICS environment, including network architecture, asset inventory, and communication protocols.

2.   **Vulnerability Scanning:** Vulnerability scanning tools are used to identify known vulnerabilities in ICS components, including SCADA systems, DCS systems, and PLCs.

3.   **Penetration Testing:** Ethical hackers conduct penetration tests to assess the security of ICS networks and devices. They simulate cyberattacks to uncover weaknesses and vulnerabilities.

4.   **Code Review:** Reviewing the code of ICS software and firmware helps identify vulnerabilities and potential security flaws.

5.   **Social Engineering Testing:** Ethical hackers test the human element of security by simulating social engineering attacks to assess the organization's resilience to such tactics.

6.   **Incident Response Testing:** Simulating incident scenarios within the ICS environment helps assess the readiness of the organization to respond to security incidents effectively.

Challenges in Ethical Hacking in ICS

Ethical hacking in ICS presents unique challenges:

1.   **Complexity:** ICS environments are highly complex, with legacy systems, proprietary protocols, and a mix of IT and OT (Operational Technology) components, making assessment and mitigation challenging.

2.   **Safety Concerns:** ICS systems often control physical processes and machinery, raising concerns about the potential impact of security testing on safety and operations.

3.   **Regulatory Compliance:** Ethical hacking in ICS must align with strict regulatory and compliance standards, requiring careful planning and documentation.

Conclusion

Ethical hacking in Industrial Control Systems (ICS) is indispensable for protecting critical infrastructure and ensuring the continued operation of essential services. As ICS environments become increasingly interconnected and digitized, the need for proactive security measures becomes more critical. By employing ethical hackers to identify vulnerabilities, assess risks, and enhance security measures, organizations can fortify the resilience of their ICS environments against an evolving landscape of cyber threats, safeguarding critical infrastructure in the digital age.

Chapter 13:

Legal and Ethical Aspects

In the ever-evolving realm of ethical hacking and cybersecurity, understanding the legal and ethical dimensions is not merely a consideration—it's an imperative. This chapter delves into the intricate intersection of law and ethics in the context of ethical hacking practices. As cybersecurity professionals navigate the complex terrain of safeguarding digital assets and combating cyber threats, they must do so within a framework that respects legal boundaries and adheres to stringent ethical principles.

Navigating the Legal Landscape

Cybersecurity, by its very nature, traverses an intricate web of laws, regulations, and statutes. From data protection laws like GDPR and HIPAA to cybercrime legislation, the legal landscape is vast and continually evolving. Ethical hackers must operate within these parameters, ensuring that their actions remain lawful, transparent, and accountable.

The Ethical Imperative

Ethical hacking carries a profound ethical responsibility.

Beyond legal compliance, ethical hackers bear the duty of safeguarding data, respecting privacy, and upholding the principles of integrity and confidentiality. This chapter explores the ethical underpinnings that guide ethical hacking practices, emphasizing the importance of trust, transparency, and responsibility.

Rules of Engagement

Rules of engagement, often defined in service-level agreements and contracts, dictate the boundaries of ethical hacking engagements. Ethical hackers must navigate these agreements meticulously, ensuring that their actions remain within the scope of authorization and adhere to predefined rules. Understanding these rules is paramount to ethical and legal compliance.

Incident Response and Legal Implications

In the event of a cybersecurity incident, incident response actions must align with both legal and ethical principles. This chapter explores the legal implications of incident response, including the obligations to report incidents, collaborate with law enforcement, and adhere to data breach notification laws.

Join us on this exploration of the legal and ethical aspects that underpin ethical hacking practices. In an era where cybersecurity is integral to safeguarding individuals, organizations, and nations, understanding the legal and ethical dimensions is not just a requisite—it's a cornerstone of responsible cybersecurity. Through diligent adherence to legal statutes and unwavering commitment to ethical principles, cybersecurity professionals can navigate the digital landscape with integrity, transparency, and the utmost responsibility.

A. Laws and Regulations: Navigating the Legal Landscape in Ethical Hacking

In the realm of ethical hacking and cybersecurity, adhering to laws and regulations is not just a best practice; it is a legal and ethical imperative. This chapter explores two pivotal regulations, the General Data Protection Regulation (GDPR) and the Health Insurance Portability and Accountability Act (HIPAA), which have profound implications for ethical hacking practices.

GDPR: Protecting Data Privacy

General Data Protection Regulation (GDPR) is a European Union regulation that came into effect in May 2018. While it primarily focuses on the protection of personal data, its global reach means that organizations worldwide must adhere to its provisions when handling the data of European Union residents.

Key Aspects of GDPR:

1.   **Data Protection by Design and Default:** GDPR mandates that organizations consider data protection principles at

the design stage of any system, including those used in ethical hacking. This ensures that privacy is a fundamental consideration.

2. **Consent:** Ethical hackers must be cognizant of the need for explicit consent when handling personal data during assessments. Data subjects must be informed about the collection, processing, and storage of their data.

3. **Data Minimization:** GDPR emphasizes the principle of data minimization, requiring organizations to collect only the data necessary for the intended purpose. Ethical hackers should follow this principle when conducting assessments.

4. **Data Subject Rights:** Individuals have rights under GDPR, including the right to access their data and the right to be forgotten. Ethical hackers must respect these rights when handling personal data.

5. **Data Breach Notification:** GDPR mandates prompt notification of data breaches to both the data protection authority and affected individuals. Ethical hackers should be aware of the legal obligations associated with data breach discovery.

HIPAA: Safeguarding Health Information

Health Insurance Portability and Accountability Act (HIPAA) is a United States federal law that regulates the handling of protected health information (PHI) by healthcare providers, health plans, and their business associates. While HIPAA primarily applies to the healthcare industry, ethical hackers conducting assessments in healthcare settings must adhere to its provisions.

Key Aspects of HIPAA:

1.   **Privacy Rule:** The HIPAA Privacy Rule governs the use and disclosure of PHI. Ethical hackers must respect the privacy of patient information and only access it as necessary for assessment purposes.

2.   **Security Rule:** The HIPAA Security Rule outlines security standards for electronic PHI (ePHI). Ethical hackers must ensure the security of ePHI during assessments and comply with the rule's requirements.

3.   **Breach Notification Rule:** HIPAA's Breach Notification Rule requires the notification of affected individuals, the U.S. Department of Health and Human Services (HHS), and, in some cases, the media, in the event of a breach of unsecured PHI.

4.   **Business Associate Agreements (BAAs):** Ethical hackers engaged by covered entities or their business associates must adhere to BAAs, which define the terms of their engagement and the protection of PHI.

Compliance in Ethical Hacking

Compliance with GDPR, HIPAA, and other relevant laws and regulations is not optional in ethical hacking. Failing to comply can result in legal consequences, financial penalties, and damage to an organization's reputation.

Ethical hackers must:

- Obtain appropriate consent when handling personal data.

- Minimize the collection of data to that which is necessary for the assessment.

- Respect data subject rights and privacy.

- Promptly report any discovered data breaches, following the legal notification process.

In summary, ethical hacking exists within a legal and ethical framework that mandates compliance with data protection laws and regulations. GDPR and HIPAA, as prime examples, impose stringent requirements that ethical hackers must adhere to when conducting assessments involving personal data and protected health information. By integrating legal and ethical considerations into their practices, ethical hackers can contribute to the responsible and lawful execution of their cybersecurity responsibilities.

B. Ethics in Ethical Hacking: Navigating the Moral Compass of Cybersecurity

Ethical hacking, as the name implies, places a strong emphasis on ethics and moral principles. In the realm of cybersecurity, where the boundaries between legal and illegal activities can sometimes blur, adhering to a strict code of ethics is fundamental. This chapter explores the ethical considerations that underpin ethical hacking, the principles that guide ethical hackers, and the importance of ethical conduct in this vital field.

Understanding the Ethical Hacker's Dilemma

Ethical hacking presents a unique dilemma for professionals in the field. On one hand, they are tasked with exploiting vulnerabilities to uncover weaknesses in systems and networks. On the other hand, they must do so responsibly, without causing harm or engaging in malicious activities. This inherent tension underscores the importance of a robust ethical framework.

Key Ethical Principles in Ethical Hacking

1. **Authorized Access:** Ethical hackers must never engage in unauthorized access to systems or networks. They should operate within the scope of authorization provided by the organization or individual who has requested their services.

2. **Consent:** Gaining informed and explicit consent from system owners or administrators is paramount. Ethical hackers

should not perform assessments without proper authorization.

3.   **Confidentiality:** Protecting sensitive information is a fundamental ethical principle. Ethical hackers should maintain the confidentiality of data they access during assessments and not disclose it to unauthorized parties.

4.   **Integrity:** Ethical hackers must conduct assessments with integrity, avoiding any actions that could damage or disrupt systems, networks, or data.

5.   **Respect for Privacy:** Respecting the privacy of individuals is essential. Ethical hackers should not invade personal privacy or collect unnecessary personal information during assessments.

6.   **Transparency and Disclosure:** Ethical hackers must provide clear and transparent communication throughout the assessment process. This includes disclosing findings, vulnerabilities, and recommendations to the organization.

7.   **Continuous Learning:** Ethical hackers should commit to continuous learning and staying up-to-date with evolving cybersecurity threats and best practices.

The Hacker's Code of Ethics

Several established codes of ethics guide ethical hacking practices, including:

- **EC-Council's Code of Ethics:** This code of ethics emphasizes integrity, confidentiality, and professional conduct for ethical hackers certified by the EC-Council.

- **(ISC)² Code of Ethics:** The (ISC)² code emphasizes protecting society, acting honorably, and providing diligent and competent service.

- **Open Web Application Security Project (OWASP) Code of Ethics:** OWASP's code focuses on the responsibility of ethical hackers to improve the security of software.

Legal and Moral Responsibility

Ethical hackers operate at the intersection of legality and morality. While they may be authorized to perform actions that could be considered malicious in other contexts, they must always act in the best interest of security and ethical conduct. Ethical hacking is a privileged position that carries significant legal and moral responsibilities.

Conclusion

Ethics in ethical hacking is not merely a consideration; it is the cornerstone of the profession. The ethical hacker's moral compass guides them through the complex landscape of cybersecurity, ensuring that their actions are responsible, lawful, and principled. By upholding ethical principles such as authorized access, consent, confidentiality, and transparency, ethical hackers play a vital role in securing digital ecosystems while fostering trust, integrity, and responsibility in the field of cybersecurity.

C. Rules of Engagement in Ethical Hacking: Defining the Boundaries of Cybersecurity Assessments

In the world of ethical hacking, success and integrity hinge upon well-defined and meticulously executed rules of engagement (RoE). These guidelines serve as the foundation for ethical hacking engagements, outlining the scope, objectives, limitations, and expectations for both ethical hackers and the organizations seeking their services. In this comprehensive exploration, we will delve into the intricacies of rules of engagement and their significance in ensuring the ethical and effective execution of cybersecurity assessments.

Defining Rules of Engagement

Rules of engagement, often abbreviated as RoE, are formal documents that delineate the terms and conditions of an ethical hacking engagement. They are negotiated and agreed upon between the organization seeking security testing and the ethical hacking team responsible for conducting the assessment. RoE serve as a contractual framework that establishes the boundaries, responsibilities, and permissions for all parties involved.

Key Components of Rules of Engagement

1.   **Scope of Work:** RoE specify the scope of the assessment, outlining the systems, networks, applications, and assets that are within the purview of the engagement. It defines what will and will not be tested.

2.   **Objectives:** The RoE document clearly defines the goals and objectives of the assessment. These objectives may include identifying vulnerabilities, assessing security controls, or testing incident response procedures.

3.   **Authorization:** Ethical hackers are explicitly granted authorization to conduct security assessments within the defined scope. This authorization is a critical component of RoE and ensures that their actions are legal and ethical.

4.   **Limitations:** RoE establish limitations on the assessment, delineating actions that are strictly prohibited. For example, limitations might include no disruption of critical services, no data exfiltration, or no unauthorized access to sensitive data.

5.   **Timing and Scheduling:** The document outlines the timeline and scheduling details for the assessment, including start and end dates, testing windows, and any downtime considerations.

6.   **Reporting Requirements:** RoE specify the format

and content of assessment reports. They detail how and when findings are to be reported, including any requirements for immediate notification of critical vulnerabilities.

7.   **Confidentiality and Data Handling:** Ethical hackers are required to handle data and findings confidentially, not disclosing any sensitive information to unauthorized parties. This section may also cover data retention and destruction policies.

8.   **Legal Compliance:** The RoE document ensures that all activities conducted during the assessment are compliant with relevant laws and regulations. It often references applicable legal frameworks and emphasizes adherence to them.

Significance of Rules of Engagement

Rules of engagement play a pivotal role in ethical hacking engagements for several reasons:

1.   **Clarity and Alignment:** RoE provide a clear and mutual understanding of the assessment's purpose, scope, and objectives, ensuring alignment between the organization and the ethical hacking team.

2.   **Legal Protection:** By explicitly granting authorization and outlining legal compliance, RoE protect both parties from potential legal issues that could arise during the engagement.

3.   **Risk Mitigation:** RoE help mitigate risks by defining

limitations and boundaries, reducing the likelihood of unintended consequences or disruptions.

4.   **Communication and Transparency:** The document promotes open communication and transparency, fostering collaboration between the organization and ethical hackers.

5.   **Accountability:** RoE establish accountability by specifying reporting requirements and timelines, ensuring that findings are promptly addressed.

Tailoring Rules of Engagement

RoE are not one-size-fits-all documents; they are tailored to each ethical hacking engagement. Different organizations, systems, and objectives require customized RoE to ensure the assessment is both effective and ethical. Ethical hackers and organizations must collaboratively craft RoE that balance the need for security testing with respect for legal and ethical boundaries.

Conclusion

Rules of engagement serve as the linchpin of ethical hacking engagements, providing a structured framework that safeguards the integrity and legality of security assessments. Ethical hackers and organizations must invest time and effort in crafting well-defined RoE to ensure that assessments are conducted professionally, responsibly, and with the utmost respect for both security and ethical principles. By doing so, they uphold the ethical and legal standards that underpin the field of ethical hacking while working collaboratively to enhance cybersecurity.

D. Incident Response and Legal Implications: Navigating the Legal Terrain of Cybersecurity Incidents

In the world of cybersecurity, the ability to respond swiftly and effectively to security incidents is paramount. However, the process of incident response carries significant legal implications that must be carefully navigated. This chapter explores the intricacies of incident response and the associated legal considerations that cybersecurity professionals, including ethical hackers, must grapple with when managing and mitigating security incidents.

Understanding Incident Response

Incident response is a systematic approach to addressing and mitigating security incidents, including breaches, data leaks, malware infections, and other cyber threats. The primary goals of incident response are to:

1.   **Identify and Confirm Incidents:** Determine whether an incident has occurred, the extent of the compromise, and the potential impact on systems, data, and operations.

2.   **Contain and Mitigate:** Take immediate actions to contain the incident and prevent further damage or data loss.

3.   **Eradicate and Recover:** Remove the threat, vulnerabilities, and traces of the incident and restore affected systems to normal operation.

4.   **Communication and Reporting:** Notify relevant parties, including stakeholders, regulatory bodies, and law enforcement, as required by law and organizational policy.

Legal Frameworks and Incident Response

Incident response operates within a complex legal landscape that varies by jurisdiction and industry. Several legal frameworks and regulations have a significant impact on how incidents are managed and reported:

1.   **Data Protection Laws (e.g., GDPR):** Regulations like the General Data Protection Regulation (GDPR) impose strict requirements for reporting data breaches. Organizations are typically required to notify supervisory authorities and affected individuals within a specified timeframe.

2.   **Industry-Specific Regulations (e.g., HIPAA):** Certain industries, such as healthcare, are subject to specific regulations governing incident response. The Health Insurance Portability and Accountability Act (HIPAA) mandates the

reporting of breaches involving protected health information (PHI).

3.   **Contractual Obligations:** Many organizations have contractual obligations with third-party vendors, clients, or partners that stipulate incident reporting requirements. Ethical hackers must be aware of these obligations.

4.   **Law Enforcement and Legal Proceedings:** In some cases, cyber incidents may lead to criminal investigations or legal proceedings. Ethical hackers may be called upon to cooperate with law enforcement, requiring careful adherence to legal procedures and obligations.

The Role of Ethical Hackers in Incident Response

Ethical hackers often play a crucial role in incident response, especially when their expertise is needed to investigate the cause of an incident, identify vulnerabilities, or assess the extent of a breach. However, they must do so within the boundaries of the law and ethical guidelines:

1.   **Legal and Ethical Conduct:** Ethical hackers must adhere to legal and ethical standards when participating in incident response activities. Unauthorized access or actions that could be perceived as malicious can have legal consequences.

2.   **Chain of Custody:** When collecting evidence during

an incident response, maintaining a secure chain of custody is essential to ensure the admissibility of evidence in legal proceedings.

3.   **Documentation:** Detailed documentation of all actions taken during incident response is critical. This documentation may be required for legal purposes and to demonstrate compliance with legal obligations.

4.   **Communication:** Effective and transparent communication with organizational stakeholders, legal counsel, and law enforcement is crucial throughout the incident response process.

Conclusion

Incident response is a fundamental aspect of cybersecurity, and ethical hackers often play a pivotal role in managing and mitigating security incidents. However, the legal implications of incident response cannot be overstated. Navigating the legal terrain requires a comprehensive understanding of relevant laws, regulations, contractual obligations, and ethical principles. Ethical hackers must operate with the utmost integrity and transparency while providing their expertise to help organizations recover from security incidents and comply with legal obligations.

Chapter 14:

Case Studies and Success Stories

In the dynamic realm of ethical hacking and cybersecurity, knowledge is not just power; it's the linchpin of success. As ethical hackers and cybersecurity professionals, the experiences of others can be invaluable in understanding real-world challenges, innovative solutions, and the ever-evolving landscape of threats. This chapter embarks on a journey through case studies and success stories, offering a glimpse into actual ethical hacking engagements, lessons learned, and the triumphs that have fortified the cybersecurity community.

The Power of Real-World Scenarios

While theories and principles lay the foundation for ethical hacking practices, nothing quite compares to the illumination provided by real-world scenarios. Case studies and success stories bring to life the challenges faced by organizations, the strategies employed to combat cyber threats, and the ultimate victories achieved. They serve as living textbooks, offering insights that transcend the theoretical and delve into the practical.

What to Expect in This Chapter

In the chapters that follow, we will delve into a curated

selection of case studies and success stories from the world of ethical hacking and cybersecurity. These narratives will encompass diverse industries, unique challenges, and innovative solutions. They will shine a light on the adaptability, resilience, and brilliance of cybersecurity professionals as they protect organizations, individuals, and critical infrastructure from the ever-persistent threat of cyberattacks.

Join us on this journey through the annals of ethical hacking, where we uncover the narratives that inspire, inform, and elevate the field of cybersecurity. Through the shared experiences of practitioners, we gain insights that not only fortify our knowledge but also reinforce our commitment to the relentless pursuit of cybersecurity excellence.

A. Real-world Ethical Hacking Engagements: Navigating the Cybersecurity Battlefield

In the ever-evolving landscape of cybersecurity, ethical hacking engagements stand as critical battlegrounds where security professionals, often referred to as ethical hackers or penetration testers, test their mettle against real-world threats. These engagements involve the simulation of cyberattacks to uncover vulnerabilities, assess security measures, and fortify digital defenses. This chapter offers a comprehensive exploration of real-world ethical hacking engagements, their methodologies, and the invaluable lessons they provide.

The Essence of Real-World Ethical Hacking Engagements

Real-world ethical hacking engagements are more than just simulations; they are immersive experiences that mirror the strategies, tactics, and vulnerabilities encountered by malicious hackers. These engagements are typically commissioned by organizations seeking to proactively identify and address security weaknesses within their systems, networks, applications, and infrastructure.

Key Aspects of Real-World Ethical Hacking Engagements

1. **Scope Definition:** Each engagement begins with a well-defined scope that outlines what will be tested and the boundaries that ethical hackers must adhere to. Scope might include specific systems, networks, or applications, and it often excludes critical or production environments to avoid disruption.

2. **Authorized Access:** Ethical hackers operate with explicit authorization from the organization. Unauthorized access is strictly prohibited, ensuring that their actions remain legal and ethical.

3. **Reconnaissance:** Ethical hackers commence engagements with reconnaissance activities, gathering information about the target environment. This phase mimics the

initial steps taken by malicious hackers to identify potential entry points.

4.   **Vulnerability Assessment:** Through systematic scanning and assessment, ethical hackers identify vulnerabilities, misconfigurations, and weaknesses within the target systems. Common tools and methodologies like vulnerability scanning, penetration testing, and code review are employed.

5.   **Exploitation and Post-Exploitation:** If vulnerabilities are identified, ethical hackers may proceed to exploit them to gain access to systems. Post-exploitation activities involve maintaining access, privilege escalation, and further exploration to understand the extent of the compromise.

6.   **Reporting and Remediation:** Ethical hackers meticulously document their findings, detailing discovered vulnerabilities, potential impacts, and recommended remediation steps. These findings are presented to the organization, which then takes action to address and mitigate the identified risks.

The Ethical Hacker's Toolbox

Ethical hackers leverage an extensive toolkit of both open-source and commercial tools and frameworks to facilitate their engagements. This toolbox includes:

- **Vulnerability Scanners:** Tools like Nessus and

OpenVAS automate vulnerability assessment by scanning systems and applications for known vulnerabilities.

- **Penetration Testing Frameworks:** Frameworks like Metasploit provide a wide array of exploits, payloads, and post-exploitation modules to test system security.

- **Password Cracking Tools:** These tools assist in testing the strength of passwords and encryption mechanisms.

- **Network Analysis Tools:** Tools like Wireshark enable ethical hackers to analyze network traffic and identify potential weaknesses.

The Lessons from Real-world Engagements

Real-world ethical hacking engagements offer invaluable lessons for both security professionals and organizations:

1. **Visibility:** Engagements provide organizations with a clear view of their security posture, helping them understand where vulnerabilities lie and where improvements are needed.

2. **Prioritization:** Ethical hackers help organizations prioritize vulnerabilities based on their severity and potential impact, ensuring that resources are allocated to address the most critical issues first.

3. **Adaptability:** Ethical hackers continuously adapt their

strategies to stay ahead of emerging threats, teaching organizations the importance of agility in cybersecurity.

4.   **Collaboration:** Effective communication between ethical hackers and organizations is paramount. Organizations benefit from the knowledge and expertise of ethical hackers, while ethical hackers rely on cooperation to achieve their goals.

Conclusion

Real-world ethical hacking engagements are not mere simulations; they are immersive experiences that replicate the tactics and threats faced by cybersecurity professionals. These engagements play a crucial role in identifying vulnerabilities, assessing security measures, and fortifying digital defenses. They serve as critical learning experiences for both ethical hackers and organizations, fostering a proactive and resilient cybersecurity ecosystem that is ever-ready to confront the relentless tide of cyber threats.

B. Lessons Learned and Best Practices: Navigating the Path to Cyber Resilience

In the dynamic and ever-evolving world of cybersecurity, learning from both success and failure is paramount. Ethical hacking, as a discipline that simulates real-world cyber threats, offers a wealth of lessons and best practices that can shape the way organizations defend against malicious actors. This chapter embarks on a comprehensive exploration of the lessons learned from ethical hacking engagements and the best practices that have emerged as a result.

The Evolving Landscape of Cyber Threats

Cyber threats are constantly evolving, becoming more sophisticated, and targeting an ever-expanding attack surface. In this context, ethical hacking engagements serve as an invaluable laboratory for understanding how adversaries operate and how defenses can be bolstered.

Key Lessons Learned

1. **Vulnerability is Inevitable:** Ethical hacking engagements often reveal that no system is impervious to vulnerabilities. The lesson here is that organizations should adopt a mindset of continuous monitoring, proactive testing, and rapid response.

2. **Defense in Depth:** A multi-layered security approach, known as defense in depth, emerges as a best practice. Relying on a single security measure is inadequate; organizations should employ multiple layers of security controls to mitigate threats.

3. **Human Factor:** The human element remains a significant vulnerability. Phishing attacks and social engineering

tactics continue to be effective, highlighting the importance of cybersecurity education and training for employees.

4.   **Patch Management:** Timely patching and updating of software and systems are critical. Ethical hackers often exploit known vulnerabilities that could have been mitigated through regular patching.

5.   **Incident Response:** The ability to respond swiftly and effectively to security incidents is a hallmark of cyber resilience. Organizations should have well-defined incident response plans and conduct regular exercises to test them.

6.   **Asset Inventory:** Maintaining an accurate inventory of all assets, including hardware and software, is essential for effective cybersecurity. Without this, critical vulnerabilities may go unnoticed.

Best Practices Emerged from Ethical Hacking

1.   **Penetration Testing:** Regular penetration testing and vulnerability assessments should be integrated into an organization's cybersecurity strategy. These tests help identify vulnerabilities before malicious actors do.

2.   **Ethical Hacking Training:** Organizations benefit from providing training and certification opportunities for their cybersecurity professionals. Ethical hacking certifications, such as

Certified Ethical Hacker (CEH) or Offensive Security Certified Professional (OSCP), are highly regarded.

3.   **Threat Intelligence:** Ethical hackers often draw insights from threat intelligence sources. Incorporating threat intelligence into security operations can enhance an organization's ability to anticipate and mitigate threats.

4.   **Zero Trust Architecture:** Zero Trust principles, where trust is never assumed and access is continuously verified, are gaining prominence. This approach minimizes the risk associated with assumed trust and lateral movement within networks.

5.   **Regular Updates and Patching:** Establishing a robust patch management process ensures that software and systems remain up to date and secure against known vulnerabilities.

6.   **Security Awareness Training:** Continuous training and awareness programs help employees recognize and report potential security threats, reducing the risk of successful social engineering attacks.

Collaboration and Sharing of Knowledge

Ethical hacking engagements have fostered a culture of collaboration and knowledge sharing within the cybersecurity community. Platforms like information sharing and analysis centers (ISACs) and online forums provide spaces for security professionals to exchange information about emerging threats and effective defense strategies.

Conclusion

Lessons learned from ethical hacking engagements and the resulting best practices have reshaped the way organizations approach cybersecurity. These experiences underscore the need for continuous vigilance, proactive testing, and a holistic approach to security. Ethical hacking, as a discipline, has not only strengthened defenses against cyber threats but has also contributed to a dynamic and resilient cybersecurity ecosystem where knowledge is shared, and collective defense is the mantra. By applying these lessons and best practices, organizations can better protect their digital assets and navigate the ever-challenging landscape of cybersecurity.

C. Ethical Hacking in Different Industries: Fortifying Cybersecurity in Specialized Ecosystems

The practice of ethical hacking transcends boundaries, adapting to the unique needs and challenges of diverse industries. From finance to healthcare, from critical infrastructure to e-commerce, ethical hackers play a pivotal role in securing digital landscapes. This chapter embarks on a comprehensive exploration of how ethical hacking is employed across different sectors, uncovering the strategies, nuances, and industry-specific considerations that define this essential cybersecurity discipline.

The Universal Need for Cybersecurity

In an increasingly interconnected world, the importance of cybersecurity knows no bounds. Cyberattacks have the potential to cripple businesses, compromise sensitive data, and even endanger lives in critical sectors. Ethical hacking, as a proactive approach to identifying and mitigating vulnerabilities, has become a cornerstone of cybersecurity strategies across industries.

Ethical Hacking in Key Industries

1. **Finance and Banking:**

- *Challenges:* The finance sector faces relentless threats from cybercriminals seeking financial gain. Ethical hackers work to secure online banking platforms, payment systems, and customer data.

- *Key Focus Areas:* Insider threats, transaction security, fraud detection, and compliance with regulations like PCI DSS.

2. **Healthcare:**

- *Challenges:* The healthcare industry is a prime target due to the value of patient data. Ethical hackers help protect electronic health records (EHRs), medical devices, and telehealth systems.

- *Key Focus Areas:* HIPAA compliance, medical device security, and safeguarding patient privacy.

3. **Critical Infrastructure:**

- *Challenges:* Critical infrastructure, including power grids and water treatment plants, is essential for society. Ethical hackers assess vulnerabilities to prevent potential disruptions.

- *Key Focus Areas:* SCADA systems security, vulnerability assessments, and resilience against cyber-physical attacks.

4. **Retail and E-commerce:**

- *Challenges:* Retailers handle vast amounts of customer data and conduct online transactions. Ethical hackers secure e-commerce platforms, point-of-sale systems, and supply chain logistics.

- *Key Focus Areas:* Payment card security (PCI DSS), data encryption, and secure online shopping experiences.

5. **Government and Defense:**

- *Challenges:* Governments face a wide range of threats, from nation-state actors to cybercriminals. Ethical hackers assess the security of government networks, military systems, and critical data.

- *Key Focus Areas:* National security, classified information protection, and compliance with government cybersecurity standards.

6. **Education:**

- *Challenges:* Educational institutions store vast amounts of sensitive student and research data. Ethical hackers help protect these assets against data breaches.

- *Key Focus Areas:* FERPA compliance (for U.S. institutions), student records security, and research data protection.

Industry-Specific Ethical Hacking Considerations

- **Regulatory Compliance:** Different industries are subject to specific regulations and standards, such as HIPAA for healthcare or GDPR for data protection in Europe. Ethical hackers must ensure that their assessments align with these requirements.

- **Business Continuity:** Some industries, like critical infrastructure, prioritize business continuity and the ability to maintain operations even in the face of cyberattacks. Ethical hacking assessments often include resilience testing.

- **Customer Trust:** In customer-centric industries like retail, maintaining customer trust is paramount. Ethical hackers help organizations avoid data breaches and cyber incidents that could erode trust.

- **Emerging Technologies:** Ethical hackers must stay abreast of industry-specific technology trends. For example, in the automotive industry, they may focus on the cybersecurity of connected vehicles.

Conclusion

Ethical hacking is not a one-size-fits-all discipline; it adapts to the unique needs and challenges of different industries. From safeguarding patient data in healthcare to protecting critical infrastructure, ethical hackers play a vital role in fortifying digital ecosystems. They serve as sentinels of cybersecurity, ensuring that organizations across various sectors are prepared to face the ever-evolving landscape of cyber threats while maintaining the trust of their stakeholders.

Conclusion

As we draw the final curtain on this journey through these pages, we invite you to reflect on the knowledge, insights, and discoveries that have unfolded before you. Our exploration of various subjects has been a captivating voyage into the depths of understanding.

In these chapters, we have ventured through the intricacies of numerous topics and examined the key concepts and findings that define these fields. It is our hope that you have found inspiration, enlightenment, and valuable takeaways that resonate with you on your own quest for knowledge.

Remember that the pursuit of understanding is an ever-evolving journey, and this book is but a milestone along the way. The world of knowledge is vast and boundless, offering endless opportunities for exploration and growth.

As you conclude this book, we encourage you to carry forward the torch of curiosity and continue your exploration of these subjects. Seek out new perspectives, engage in meaningful discussions, and embrace the thrill of lifelong learning.

We express our sincere gratitude for joining us on this intellectual adventure. Your curiosity and dedication to expanding your horizons are the driving forces behind our shared quest for wisdom and insight.

Thank you for entrusting us with a portion of your intellectual journey. May your pursuit of knowledge lead you to new heights and inspire others to embark on their own quests for understanding.

With profound gratitude,

Nikhilesh Mishra, Author

Recap of Key Takeaways

As we near the culmination of our journey through the realm of ethical hacking, it is essential to pause and reflect on the valuable insights, lessons, and best practices that have been unveiled along the way. The path we have treaded is not merely a collection of knowledge; it is a compendium of wisdom—an arsenal of principles and practices that fortify the cybersecurity domain. This section serves as a comprehensive recapitulation of the key takeaways, distilling them into pillars upon which the future of ethical hacking stands.

1. Cybersecurity Fundamentals: The Bedrock of Ethical Hacking

- Ethical hacking begins with a firm grasp of cybersecurity fundamentals, including understanding threats, vulnerabilities, and the importance of the CIA Triad (Confidentiality, Integrity, Availability).

2. Ethical Hacking Methodology: A Structured Approach

- Ethical hacking follows a structured methodology encompassing reconnaissance, scanning, vulnerability assessment, exploitation, post-exploitation, and reporting.

3. Real-World Engagement: The Crucible of Learning

- Real-world ethical hacking engagements provide

invaluable insights into the ever-evolving tactics and strategies of malicious actors, highlighting the importance of proactive cybersecurity measures.

4. Defense in Depth: A Multilayered Strategy

- The concept of defense in depth emphasizes the importance of employing multiple layers of security controls to safeguard against cyber threats.

5. Compliance and Regulations: Legal Frameworks

- Ethical hackers must operate within the boundaries of legal and regulatory frameworks, including GDPR, HIPAA, and industry-specific standards.

6. Collaboration and Sharing: A Community United

- Knowledge sharing and collaboration within the cybersecurity community are pivotal in staying ahead of emerging threats and fostering a culture of collective defense.

7. Cyber Resilience: Preparing for the Unpredictable

- Cyber resilience entails not only preventing cyberattacks but also having robust incident response plans and business continuity strategies.

8. Education and Training: A Continuous Journey

- Cybersecurity professionals, including ethical hackers, benefit from ongoing education and training to keep pace with evolving threats and technologies.

9. Adaptability and Innovation: Staying Ahead

- Ethical hackers must continuously adapt their strategies and embrace innovative tools and techniques to outwit evolving cyber threats.

10. Trust and Integrity: The Ethical Hacker's Code

- Ethical hackers must operate with the utmost trustworthiness, transparency, and integrity, adhering to the principles of responsible disclosure.

Conclusion: Forging Ahead

As we conclude this voyage through the ethical hacking odyssey, we are reminded that the journey is far from over. Ethical hacking is a dynamic and relentless pursuit—a commitment to defending the digital realm. The key takeaways from our exploration serve as guiding lights, illuminating the path forward in a landscape where cyber threats are ever-advancing and the need for ethical hacking remains paramount.

Our collective mission is clear: to safeguard digital ecosystems, fortify data fortresses, and advance the boundaries of cyber resilience. As we venture forth, let us carry these takeaways as our armor and our compass—a compass that directs us toward a future where ethical hacking remains a beacon of hope and a shield against the relentless tide of cyber threats.

In the digital age, the battle for cybersecurity knows no boundaries. With the knowledge gained, the principles embraced, and the spirit of ethical hacking as our ally, we forge ahead—undaunted and resolute—knowing that the challenges may be formidable, but our determination to protect, defend, and secure is unwavering.

The Future of Ethical Hacking

As we stand on the precipice of the digital age, where innovation and connectivity propel us into uncharted territories, the role of ethical hacking is poised to evolve in lockstep with the ever-expanding threat landscape. The future of ethical hacking is a landscape of promise and challenge—a realm where cybersecurity professionals, armed with knowledge, adaptability, and a commitment to ethics, will continue to stand as the vanguards of digital defense.

Emerging Trends and Paradigm Shifts

1. **AI and Machine Learning in Ethical Hacking:**

   - Ethical hackers will increasingly harness the power of artificial intelligence and machine learning to analyze vast datasets, detect anomalies, and identify potential threats in real time. These technologies will enable more proactive and precise threat hunting.

2. **Automation of Ethical Hacking:**

   - The automation of routine ethical hacking tasks, such as vulnerability scanning and basic exploitation, will free up human ethical hackers to focus on complex, strategic, and creative aspects of cybersecurity.

3. **IoT and Industrial Control System (ICS) Security:**

- The proliferation of Internet of Things (IoT) devices and the integration of digital technologies into critical infrastructure will necessitate specialized ethical hacking skills to secure these interconnected systems.

4. **Cloud Security Challenges:**

- Ethical hackers will grapple with securing cloud environments, including identifying misconfigurations, data leakage, and ensuring compliance with evolving cloud security standards.

5. **Zero Trust Architecture:**

- The adoption of Zero Trust principles, where trust is never assumed, will drive the need for ethical hackers to assess and reinforce continuous verification and access control mechanisms.

6. **Quantum Computing Threats:**

- The advent of quantum computing will introduce new challenges in cryptography and encryption. Ethical hackers will need to explore post-quantum cryptographic solutions and assess their vulnerabilities.

7. **Cybersecurity Regulations:**

- As governments worldwide enact stricter cybersecurity regulations, ethical hackers will play a crucial role in ensuring compliance and helping organizations navigate the legal and ethical aspects of cybersecurity.

Challenges on the Horizon

1. **Advanced Threat Actors:**

- As ethical hacking evolves, so do the tactics of malicious actors. Nation-state-sponsored cyberattacks and highly sophisticated threat actors will continue to pose significant challenges.

2. **Privacy Concerns:**

- Ethical hackers must navigate the ethical dilemma of privacy, particularly in the context of offensive security practices, while balancing the imperative of uncovering vulnerabilities.

3. **Skills Shortage:**

- The demand for skilled ethical hackers is outpacing the supply. Bridging this skills gap will be crucial for organizations to stay resilient against cyber threats.

4. **Legal and Ethical Gray Areas:**

- Emerging technologies and cyber conflict scenarios may blur the lines between ethical and unethical hacking. Clear ethical guidelines and legal frameworks will be essential.

The Ethical Hacker of Tomorrow

The ethical hacker of the future will be a multidisciplinary expert—a combination of technical virtuosity, creative problem-solving, and an unwavering commitment to ethics. These professionals will need to adapt to emerging technologies, master automation and AI tools, and become proficient in securing diverse ecosystems, from IoT to cloud to quantum-resistant cryptography.

Conclusion

The future of ethical hacking is a dynamic and challenging landscape, where the battle for cybersecurity knows no boundaries. The ethical hacker of tomorrow will be at the forefront of this digital battleground, standing as the sentinel of digital defense, adapting to evolving threats, and fortifying the foundations of a safer digital world.

As we embrace the future, let us do so with the conviction that the principles of integrity, transparency, and ethical conduct will continue to guide our path. The challenges may be formidable, but the ethical hacker's resolve remains unwavering—steadfast in the pursuit of securing the digital age and navigating the ever-evolving cyber battleground of tomorrow.

Glossary of Terms

1. **Ethical Hacking:** The practice of probing computer systems, networks, and applications for security vulnerabilities, with the authorization to do so, to identify weaknesses before malicious hackers can exploit them.

2. **Vulnerability:** A flaw or weakness in a system's security that could potentially be exploited by an attacker to compromise the system's integrity, availability, or confidentiality.

3. **Penetration Testing:** A controlled and authorized simulation of a cyberattack against a system or network to evaluate its security, identify vulnerabilities, and assess its resistance to attacks.

4. **Exploit:** A specific technique or piece of code that takes advantage of a vulnerability to gain unauthorized access or control over a system.

5. **Zero-Day Vulnerability:** A security flaw in software or hardware that is unknown to the vendor and remains unpatched, making it a potential target for cyberattacks.

6. **Firewall:** A network security device or software that filters incoming and outgoing network traffic based on predefined security rules, helping protect a network from unauthorized access and threats.

7. **Intrusion Detection System (IDS):** A security tool that monitors network traffic for suspicious or malicious activity and alerts administrators when potential threats are detected.

8. **Intrusion Prevention System (IPS):** A security tool that not only detects suspicious activity but also takes automated actions to prevent or block potential threats in real-time.

9. **Phishing:** A social engineering attack where cybercriminals impersonate a legitimate entity to trick individuals into revealing sensitive information, such as passwords or credit card numbers.

10. **Malware:** Malicious software designed to infiltrate, damage, or gain unauthorized access to computer systems. Types of malware include viruses, worms, Trojans, and ransomware.

11. **Denial of Service (DoS) Attack:** An attack in which an attacker overwhelms a target system or network with excessive traffic or requests, causing it to become unavailable to legitimate users.

12. **Distributed Denial of Service (DDoS) Attack:** Similar to a DoS attack but involves multiple compromised computers (botnets) working together to flood a target with traffic, making it harder to mitigate.

13. **Social Engineering:** Manipulative techniques used to deceive

individuals into divulging confidential information or performing actions that compromise security.

14. **Cryptography:** The practice of encoding information to secure it from unauthorized access, with techniques such as encryption and decryption.

15. **Encryption:** The process of converting plaintext (readable data) into ciphertext (unreadable data) using algorithms and keys, making it secure during transmission or storage.

16. **Decryption:** The process of converting ciphertext back into plaintext using the appropriate decryption key.

17. **Public Key Infrastructure (PKI):** A system of cryptographic elements, including public and private keys, certificates, and digital signatures, used to secure communication and authenticate users.

18. **Brute Force Attack:** An attack method in which an attacker systematically tries all possible combinations of passwords or encryption keys until the correct one is found.

19. **Patch:** A software update or fix released by a vendor to address security vulnerabilities or bugs in their software or operating systems.

20. **Incident Response:** The process of managing and mitigating the impact of a cybersecurity incident, including identifying,

containing, eradicating, and recovering from the incident.

This glossary provides a foundational understanding of key terms in the world of ethical hacking. Ethical hackers must continuously expand their knowledge of these terms and stay updated with evolving terminology to effectively navigate the complex and dynamic field of cybersecurity.

Resources and References

As you reach the final pages of this book by Nikhilesh Mishra, consider it not an ending but a stepping stone. The pursuit of knowledge is an unending journey, and the world of information is boundless.

Discover a World Beyond These Pages

We extend a warm invitation to explore a realm of boundless learning and discovery through our dedicated online platform: **www.nikhileshmishra.com**. Here, you will unearth a carefully curated trove of resources and references to empower your quest for wisdom.

Unleash the Potential of Your Mind

- **Digital Libraries:** Immerse yourself in vast digital libraries, granting access to books, research papers, and academic treasures.

- **Interactive Courses:** Engage with interactive courses and lectures from world-renowned institutions, nurturing your thirst for knowledge.

- **Enlightening Talks:** Be captivated by enlightening talks delivered by visionaries and experts from diverse fields.

- **Community Connections:** Connect with a global community of like-minded seekers, engage in meaningful discussions, and share your knowledge journey.

Your Journey Has Just Begun

Your journey as a seeker of knowledge need not end here. Our website awaits your exploration, offering a gateway to an infinite universe of insights and references tailored to ignite your intellectual curiosity.

Acknowledgments

As I stand at this pivotal juncture, reflecting upon the completion of this monumental work, I am overwhelmed with profound gratitude for the exceptional individuals who have been instrumental in shaping this remarkable journey.

In Loving Memory

To my father, **Late Shri Krishna Gopal Mishra,** whose legacy of wisdom and strength continues to illuminate my path, even in his physical absence, I offer my deepest respect and heartfelt appreciation.

The Pillars of Support

My mother, **Mrs. Vijay Kanti Mishra,** embodies unwavering resilience and grace. Your steadfast support and unwavering faith in my pursuits have been the bedrock of my journey.

To my beloved wife, **Mrs. Anshika Mishra,** your unshakable belief in my abilities has been an eternal wellspring of motivation. Your constant encouragement has propelled me to reach new heights.

My daughter, **Miss Aarvi Mishra,** infuses my life with boundless joy and unbridled inspiration. Your insatiable curiosity serves as a constant reminder of the limitless power of exploration and discovery.

Brothers in Arms

To my younger brothers, **Mr. Ashutosh Mishra** and **Mr. Devashish Mishra,** who have steadfastly stood by my side, offering unwavering support and shared experiences that underscore the strength of familial bonds.

A Journey Shared

This book is a testament to the countless hours of dedication and effort that have gone into its creation. I am immensely grateful for the privilege of sharing my knowledge and insights with a global audience.

Readers, My Companions

To all the readers who embark on this intellectual journey alongside me, your curiosity and unquenchable thirst for knowledge inspire me to continually push the boundaries of understanding in the realm of cloud computing.

With profound appreciation and sincere gratitude,

Nikhilesh Mishra

September 08, 2023

About the Author

Nikhilesh Mishra is an extraordinary visionary, propelled by an insatiable curiosity and an unyielding passion for innovation. With a relentless commitment to exploring the boundaries of knowledge and technology, Nikhilesh has embarked on an exceptional journey to unravel the intricate complexities of our world.

Hailing from the vibrant and diverse landscape of India, Nikhilesh's pursuit of knowledge has driven him to plunge deep into the world of discovery and understanding from a remarkably young age. His unwavering determination and quest for innovation have not only cemented his position as a thought leader but have also earned him global recognition in the ever-evolving realm of technology and human understanding.

Over the years, Nikhilesh has not only mastered the art of translating complex concepts into accessible insights but has also crafted a unique talent for inspiring others to explore the limitless possibilities of human potential.

Nikhilesh's journey transcends the mere boundaries of expertise; it is a transformative odyssey that challenges conventional wisdom and redefines the essence of exploration. His commitment to pushing the boundaries and reimagining the norm serves as a luminous beacon of inspiration to all those who aspire to make a profound impact in the world of knowledge.

As you navigate the intricate corridors of human understanding and innovation, you will not only gain insight into Nikhilesh's expertise but also experience his unwavering dedication to empowering readers like you. Prepare to be enthralled as he seamlessly melds intricate insights with real-world applications, igniting the flames of curiosity and innovation within each reader.

Nikhilesh Mishra's work extends beyond the realm of authorship; it is a reflection of his steadfast commitment to shaping the future of knowledge and exploration. It is an embodiment of his boundless dedication to disseminating wisdom for the betterment of individuals worldwide.

Prepare to be inspired, enlightened, and empowered as you embark on this transformative journey alongside Nikhilesh Mishra. Your understanding of the world will be forever enriched, and your passion for exploration and innovation will reach new heights under his expert guidance.

Sincerely, **A Fellow Explorer**

Notes

Notes

Notes